CUSTOM CARS & LEAD SLEDS

America's Best Customs 50's—90's

Timothy Remus

Motorbooks International
Publishers & Wholesalers ®

First published in 1990 by Motorbooks International Publishers & Wholesalers, P O Box 2, 729 Prospect Avenue, Osceola, WI 54020 USA

Motorbooks International books are also available at discounts in bulk quantity for industrial or sales-promotional use. For details write to Special Sales Manager at the Publisher's address

Library of Congress Cataloging-in-Publication Data
Remus, Timothy.
    Custom cars and lead sleds / Timothy Remus.
        p. cm.
    ISBN 0-87938-424-7(soft)
    1. Automobiles—Customizing.   I. Title.
TL154.R45 1990   90-35480
629.28′72—dc20   CIP

Printed and bound in Hong Kong

On the front cover: *Porky's drive-in in Des Moines, Iowa, is a popular cruise during Last Pass, the season-ending event organized by the Kustom Kemp group. In the foreground is the flame-covered '50 Ford owned by James Gaedke of Colo, Iowa. In the background is the flamed '49 Mercury* Rebel Rouser *and blue '55 Ford* Sweet Child. *Fran Mansell of Independence, Missouri, leans on the '50 Ford in her poodle skirt; her husband, F. R. Mansell, is in the red coat in the background.*

On the back cover: *The custom '51 Mercury owned by Bob Schuh of St. Cloud, Minnesota. Finished in 1988, the car is photographed against a Minneapolis, Minnesota, skyscraper, emphasizing the car's looks.*

On the frontispiece: *'50 Oldsmobile fastback custom* Bad Boy II *owned by "Big George" Greenwalt of Grant, Florida, with Frenched antenna slots.*

On the title page: *Two classics of the custom car era, the* Rod & Custom *magazine's project* Dream Truck *and Sam Barris' Buick. Both customs are owned today by Kurt McCormick of St. Louis, Missouri.*

Contents

Acknowledgments

Like most big projects this one couldn't have been done alone. There are a number of people to thank.

First, there are the car owners. While I realize they all want their car to appear in a book or magazine, some went to considerable lengths to accommodate me and my camera. In particular I have to thank Doug and Nita Thompson, and Kurt McCormick. Each made available to me their extensive collections of early magazines and each did proofreading of various sections of the book. Without the information they made available to me the book would have been much more difficult to put together.

I have to thank Jerry Titus from KKOA for much the same reasons and for extending his hospitality to me whenever I showed up at one of his events.

Dean Batchelor, source of at least one great nostalgic article in a recent issue of *Rod & Custom*, provided some excellent pictures taken in the early days of custom cars. The pictures, seen in the first chapter, provide a certain feeling that couldn't have been accomplished in any other way.

Finally there's Frank Kaino. Frank provided some critical encouragement to a young, fledgling motorhead/journalist some years back. Without it projects like this might never have happened.

Introduction

It's all Butch's fault. Butch is the one who invited me to the monthly meeting of the local KKOA club early in 1987. And Butch is the one who got me to Last Pass, the annual custom car event held in Des Moines, Iowa, each year.

But this book started long before that. It started in Marlo's backyard during my early high school years. Marlo was three or four years older than me—old enough to have a car of his own. Marlo and friends were always lying under their '50 Fords and I became the self-appointed "go-fer."

I learned a lot of things at Marlo's. Like how to identify a 9/16 combination wrench, how to get ungodly dirty and how to cuss like the big kids. The year was 1962 and the cars that Marlo worked on might have been called mild customs.

Eventually Marlo went into the Army and I moved. By the time I had a car of my own there were more tempting delights than flathead Ford convertibles. The Beach Boys sang of Chevrolet 409s and close on its heels (and with its own song) came the first true factory hot rod, the Pontiac GTO. Marlo's tail-dragging Ford was soon forgotten as I dreamed Tri-Power Pontiacs and big-block, wedge Mopars. Horsepower was hot and customs weren't even cool.

When the muscle cars died in the mid 1970s, nearly everything automotive died with them. Ten years later, when the renaissance of things automotive was starting to roll along I was involved in the publication of a small motorcycle magazine. As the rebirth picked up steam it seemed all my friends had their old street rods and street machines out of the garage and back on the street again.

The smell of high octane was in the air and I suggested to my partner (I still can't believe this) that we start a new, locally based street rod and high-performance magazine. One thing led to another, Butch called and it all seemed to connect. Soon I was going to every custom event in the Midwest with a box of magazines and a small table.

I discovered two things: First, customs are neat. Second, the cars are neat because they're built by enthusiastic people. The enthusiasm these people show for anything custom is total and contagious. Before long I became the dedicated custom guy on our staff, writing all the custom car features.

At the time there wasn't much being written on customs. *Rod & Custom* magazine hadn't come back and Tex Smith hadn't started his custom magazine. Yet there were all these custom fans with a hunger for information. It seemed that satisfying that hunger would take more than a few magazine articles.

This book is intended to answer that need for more information. The information presented here is both technical—in terms of how a car was conceived and built—and anecdotal. Just as important as the source of a toothed grille or the size of an engine is the owner's reasons for building the car—his or her source of enthusiasm.

The cars themselves range from old to new; from the Sam Barris Buick built in 1953, to Ray and Myrna's *Plum Wild* Buick built in 1988. They all tend toward the traditional, and even those built in the last few years reflect what I think are the best attributes of the 1950s cars.

How did I pick the cars? How did I choose fourteen cars from the thousands that were displayed at the various events? Besides a tendency toward tradition, I looked for cars with good energy; cars that display the enthusiasm of their owners. While some are more beautiful than others or better crafted, they all say, "Customs are exciting, customs are fun."

There's one more thing they all have in common: I like 'em.

Porky's drive-in, Des Moines, Iowa, opposite. The '50 Ford in the foreground is owned by James Gaedke of Colo, Iowa. In the background is the '49 Mercury Rebel Rouser *and the '55 Ford* Sweet Child. *Fran Mansell of Independence, Missouri, leans on the door of the '50 Ford while her husband, F. R. Mansell, stands in the background.*

Customs Then and Now

From boom to bust— and back to boom

Custom cars might seem the product of those wonderful, nostalgic 1950s—that postwar period known for poodle skirts and the birth of rock-and-roll. Actually, custom cars existed before 1950. In fact, there have always been custom cars, "custom" meaning simply a car that has been changed from stock. In the earliest days coachbuilders put their own bodies on a Ford, Packard or Cadillac chassis. There

were Brewster Fords and Darren Packards. The cars themselves were usually built for wealthy individuals who needed something different, a sexier car with added prestige.

Coachbuilders like Brunn, LeBaron and Dietrich, and Bohman & Schwartz built beautiful cars with graceful, flowing lines. Their work was flawless, the designs superb. There was only one problem: cost. Not only was the coachbuilding expensive, the Packards, Lincolns and Cadillacs that were most often modified were expensive cars to start with.

The first customs might be considered coachbuilt cars for the masses. The difference was in the price. Building a custom was never cheap. However, the cost of a custom built in one of the small shops, using a Ford or Chevy as the basis, would eat up a working man's wages.

Customs as we know them really got started after the war and by the mid 1950s it seemed every young man wanted a custom car: a Ford or a Merc with all the chrome removed, a chopped top and as low to the ground as possible. The newsstand was full of car magazines. Many of these magazines measured only 5 x 8 inches (the little magazines) and all of them were filled with the hottest stuff from the West Coast. In between the car features, most magazines carried how-to articles explaining ways the reader could duplicate those wonderful customs in his own garage.

In spite of the overwhelming popularity of customs, by the middle of the 1960s they were gone. The shoebox Fords and James Dean Mercurys were relegated to a dusty corner of the garage or buried under tarps in the back of the body shop. In order to understand how this phenomena of custom car fever became so quickly popular and faded just as quickly, it's necessary to step back in time for a short history lesson.

The 1940s: Hot rods for speed, customs for looks

It happened on the West Coast and it started before the war. Car fever was an entrenched disease

Porky's drive-in, Des Moines, Iowa, keeps the 1950s custom style alive. Parked alongside a 1960s Ford Mustang rests a '57 Oldsmobile custom.

There have always been custom cars—custom meaning simply a car that has been changed from stock

in California. The combination of great weather, a growing population and the availability of the dry lakes for speed contests made California the heart of an evolving car culture. The streets were full of modified cars: Ford roadsters with souped up engines, and Chevy coupes with skirts and chopped tops. Car guys were either into hot rods for speed or customs for looks. On weekends there was cruising to the drive-in at night and hanging out at the dry lakes during the day.

While the custom guys were concerned more with style than speed, there was considerable cross-pollination between the two groups. The dry lakes near Los Angeles had been popular for speed trials since the 1930s. Participants learned early that a chopped top offered less wind resistance and thus raised a car's top speed. Other early aerodynamic treatments followed: full skirts on the rear, removal of the bumpers and filled fender seams.

The first true customs were built either at home or in conventional body shops for special customers or employees. By the late 1940s, however, there was enough demand for custom work to support some small custom-only shops. One of the first to make the crossover from coachbuilding to customs was Harry Westergard. Harry was known as a restylist and ran a small backyard shop in Sacramento, California.

The Westergard look often depicted is a mid 1930s coupe, low to the ground with filled hood sides, a tall, narrow grille, fender skirts and fade-away rear sheet metal. The overall effect is much like a teardrop, big in front and diminishing toward the rear.

Harry had a protégé, a young man who hung around the shop after school. In time Harry took a liking to the boy and began to show him some of the finer points of leading fenders or recessing a license plate. Eventually the young man became a part-time employee in Harry's shop. The welding, painting and layout lessons that this young man learned would serve him well later when he opened a custom shop of his own.

The young man's name was George Barris. He eventually moved to Los Angeles where he got a job in a body shop. When brother Sam returned from the

Navy in 1946, George proposed they open a custom shop of their own. Their first shop was quite small, located at Imperial Avenue in Los Angeles.

George was the body man, but Sam was eager to learn. Their first years were a little lean but by 1948 they were doing steady business and in 1949 they took home a trophy from the first Oakland Roadster show.

With the end of the war thousands of young men came home through California. Many of those men never left the Golden state. Those that stayed seemed to think a distinctive set of wheels was essential and most were willing to spend a high percentage of their wages to achieve that end. Some of these men achieved distinction by having the fastest (so they said) car on the street. Those individuals spent their extra earnings on twin-carb manifolds and Offenhauser high-compression heads. For others, the look of their ride was most important. Achieving the right look was often accomplished in one of the small California custom shops. There were enough early custom enthusiasts to keep a surprisingly large number of custom shops busy.

By the late 1940s Sam and George had moved into their second, larger shop and business was booming. The Barris brothers weren't alone. On the east side of Los Angeles there was Gil Ayala's shop and in Burbank, Neil Emory and Clayton Jensen ran a small shop known as Valley Custom. Farther north Gene Winfield ran Windy's Custom Shop in Modesto and Joe Bailon worked from his shop in Hayward.

Early 1950s: Debut of the great Mercury

Most of the early customs were subtle. Usually the customizer, or restylist, stayed close to the Detroit rendering. The chrome was often removed, license plates and taillights were Frenched or set into the body. Cars were lowered, often by adding lowering blocks in the rear between the spring and the axle, and cutting a coil or two from the front springs. Chopped tops were cut only a few inches; the end result was anything but radical.

As the first of the truly new postwar car designs came out, some of the better known shops took on the challenge of working in virgin territory—customizing new designs that had never been altered.

One of the most popular cars from a customizer's standpoint was the new Mercury design, which made its debut in 1949. One of the first shops to tackle the job of customizing the Merc was that of the Barris brothers. In 1952 they built a '51 Merc for Bob Hirohata. The Hirohata Merc went on to win first

El Mirage dry lake, 1946. Earle Bruce's '40 Ford coupe shows early "aero" treatment: chopped top, fender skirts *and filled quarter windows. Note removal of chrome, running boards and door handles.* Dean Batchelor

place trophies at every show.

The Hirohata car created a sensation unlike any other car up to that time. It was featured in the movie *Running Wild*. Soon, every kid from California to Connecticut wanted a Merc with a chopped top and a Caddy mill. Hollywood helped too: Everyone's favorite rebel, James Dean, who made only three movies, drove a 1950 Merc in *Rebel Without a Cause*. The fate of Mercs was sealed forever—like James Dean, the '49-'51 Merc would go on to cult status.

Mid 1950s: Designs evolve through car shows and competition

As the better known shops gained experience new techniques were introduced. Valley Custom is thought to be the first shop to do a sectioning job, taking a thin strip of metal out of the car all the way around. Gene Winfield created a bullet grille. Paint got wilder, too. Joe Bailon introduced Candy Apple hues created by using a gold or silver underbase. Pinstripes weren't enough anymore and gave way to scallops.

Circa 1941. This '36 Ford coupe has the right look: chopped top, tall narrow grille and fender skirts in back. Dean Batchelor

By the mid 1950s the designs were moving rapidly past the early, conservative work of the first custom shops. Fueled in part by the car show circuit, the Barris brothers, Ayala's shop, Valley Custom, Bailon, Winfield and many others were competing for trophies at the car shows. It seemed too easy for a judge to walk past a subtle, clean custom. Most of the shops began turning out cars designed for the show. Cars were built to appeal to the judges. The car magazines followed and were soon filled with "show" customs, cars like the '55 Chev built by the Barris brothers in the late 1950s, with a small TV, bar and phone built in.

None of the special equipment worked; it was all intended for show—to win a trophy.

During this same period another kind of car show was very popular: the new car show held in the winter in most cities. Along with all the new and wonderful cars there were the idea or concept cars, cars with fins and airplane-like, futuristic styling. These cars helped fuel the accelerating trend toward exotic customs.

Late 1950s: Wilder and wilder

Pushed by intense car show competition, inspired by new designs and concept cars from Detroit, and with new tools like fiberglass and plastic body filler, the customs of the late 1950s took on a look all their own. There were new names on the trophies as well. Men like Darryl Starbird, Bill Cushenberry, Ray Farhner and Doug Thompson turned out designs much wilder than the more subtle work that went before.

If custom fans from 1958 thought Joe Bailon's *Mystery Ford* or Darryl Starbird's *Predicta* (with its bubble top) were wild, well, they hadn't seen nothing yet! Enter Ed "Big Daddy" Roth and Dean Jeffries, two individuals who started out as pinstripers and ended as cult heroes.

In 1959 Ed Roth (the Big Daddy title came later) unveiled *Outlaw*, a Bucket T unlike any Bucket T seen before. In place of the traditional Ford grille shell, Ed fabricated his own nose piece with an invisible radiator and quad lights. Soon to follow was *Beatnik Bandit*, a wild bubble top show car with wild scallops on a creme paint job.

It got wilder and wilder until the show car became a carriage powered by a blown Chrysler hemi. Soon there was hardly any car at all—just a fiberglass rendering of something, almost anything—and a big hairy motor.

The 1960s: Decline and fall

Some say it was the evolution of the cars, from Mercurys with chopped tops and cruiser skirts to Hemi-powered caskets built just for show. From cars that resembled the one you had at home to vehicles that might not even run. Others say it was the new factory hot rods from Detroit, the 409 Impala and later the GTO. Cars that had lots of show and more than enough go. Whatever the cause, by the mid 1960s, customs were dead. So dead that the Hirohata Merc, custom to end all customs, was seen in the back row of a used car lot with a $300 price tag in the window.

But the custom movement wasn't really dead—only taking a rest of sorts. The revival of customs would take nearly fifteen years and a lot of energy

A '55 Chevrolet as built by George Barris in the late 1950s. Note the radical change in styling from the smooth, clean customs of the early 1950s.

from enthusiastic people. People like die-hard custom fan Jerry Titus who held the Merc-Deuce reunion in 1979. Intended to get together the best of the old hot rod and custom movements from years gone by, Jerry planned a big blast at the drag strip in Kansas City. Instead of thousands of enthusiasts, Jerry and his helpers got only 300 participants.

The 1980s: Born again

Broke but not broken, Jerry Titus used the mailing list from the Merc-Deuce reunion and sent out a questionnaire. Using the results of the questionnaire as a guideline, Jerry began to think of an organization based solely on customs. In September of 1980 Jerry placed an ad in the Wichita, Kansas, newspaper inviting any interested custom fans to meet with him on the first of October.

Fourteen couples showed up. It may not sound like much of a success but those fourteen were the core group of a new organization, Kustom Kemps of America.

In 1981 they held their first nationals attracting 383 participants. One year later 600 of the true believers dusted off their old customs for the second Lead Sled Spectacular. Most of these people were the kids of the 1950s grown a little older and a little wiser: men who saved for a '50 Ford or '51 Merc with a flathead V-8, women who wore poodle skirts to high school.

Joe Bailon's well-known custom shop as it appeared in the mid 1950s. Dean Batchelor

Another Bailon custom, a '50 Ford owned by Elton Kantor. A true tail-dragging custom. The picture dates from about 1952. Dean Batchelor

Darryl Starbird's Predicta *with its bubble top, built during the days of wild, non-functional custom cars.*

By 1988 it was apparent this custom phenomena was more than just the nostalgic dreams of some jaded old-timers. The 1988 Lead Sled Spectacular was held in August in Holland, Michigan. When the show opened officially on Friday morning it was apparent this would be the best KKOA event ever. Attendance was up, the road leading through the fairgrounds was crowded with vendors and the organization of the show was top-notch. The cars pulling through the gate were the best anyone remembered seeing. Some of the cars were still those same unfinished or refurbished sleds from the owners' high school days. Others were brand new, finished just before the event.

Parked in the shade of the trees were some real show stoppers. Jack Walker brought the Hirohata Merc replica, a beautiful copy of the Merc that appeared on so many magazine covers in 1953. Built in 1985 by Doug Thompson in Kansas City, the Hirohata Merc replica was a direct link with the roots of the custom movement. Under another tree was the hit of the show, a '51 Buick known as *Plum Wild*. *Plum Wild* was designed by M. K. John and built by Merlin Berg in Berg's small Iowa shop. Originally a four-door, the Buick appeared minus two of those doors, with a Carson top and a shape that can only be called long, low and beautiful. Finished just before the show, *Plum Wild* drew crowds all weekend. The strength of the cars and the enthusiasm of the participants proved to one and all that customs are here to stay.

The future

What does the future hold? It seems safe to predict more growth. While there may be a diminishing supply of clean '50 Mercurys, there is an enormous number of clean 1950s cars just waiting for someone to knock off the door handles and maybe cut a coil or two. Parts that are hard to find, like DeSoto grilles, are being reproduced.

The most important ingredient, of course, is the people. As more and more of the baby boomers reach a point in their life where they can take a little more time off, more and more will discover their automotive roots. For many, those roots are spelled C-U-S-T-O-M.

When customs disappeared in the 1960s these individuals went on to adult pursuits—things like raising children, securing careers and building businesses. Now, twenty years later, their children are mostly grown, their careers are secure and their businesses allow weekends away. And despite a little grey hair, these people are still kids of the 1950s.

From its meager beginnings Kustom Kemps of America (KKOA) has grown year by year. There were some tough times, like 1984 when a fancy magazine proved too expensive. Restructuring was in order and a smaller, less glossy *KKOA Gazette* resulted. Growth of the organization has continued, with each event drawing a few more cars than the one before.

The crowded scene at the Lead Sled Spectacular 1988. By 1988 it was apparent that the rebirth of custom cars was more than just a short-lived fad.

Sam Barris Buick

The master builds one for himself

The story of the '50 Buick seen here really starts in 1945. That was the year Sam Barris agreed to join brother George in the custom business. George had been working in a small custom/body shop in the Los Angeles area and when Sam was discharged from the Navy late in 1945, George suggested they go into the custom car business together.

George was the master, the customizer and body man who had to teach brother Sam the trade. If there has ever been any doubt that Sam learned well and became a master in his own right, this car should erase those doubts.

The Buick was almost new when Sam acquired it. He found it in a junkyard following a garage fire. The car was totaled and Sam got it cheap. With a couple of tires and a hot-wired ignition, Sam was able to drive it back to the shop. The Buick was parked in the back corner of the Barris shop where Sam could spend evenings and weekends working on it—the Buick was to be Sam's very own, personal custom.

Once in the shop, Sam stripped the Buick of its southern fried interior and removed all the exterior trim. The plan for the Buick was both modest and grand. Modest in the sense that the finished car would be a subtle custom, with clean, graceful lines and not a hint of gaudiness. At the same time Sam's plan was revolutionary because the modifications, especially a top chop on a fastback, would be quite difficult to perform.

After stripping the body of its trim, Sam started on the top. The Barris cars are known for their tapering line, falling off toward the rear. Sam wanted more than just a chopped top, he wanted the top lower in the rear and he wanted to keep both the stock fastback lines and the original rear window.

First, it was necessary to remove the entire rear window and its framework. Next, the trunk lid and doors were removed. Finally, Sam could begin the actual work of cutting the roof. At the front the windshield posts were cut 3½ inches. At the rear the top was dropped 5½ inches by removing metal from the inner trunk and deck lid.

Once the top was roughed in, the original rear window could be remounted at an almost horizontal angle. Next, the doors were cut to match the new roof line. Because the rear of the roof now came down into what used to be the trunk, the trunk lid had to be cut and reshaped to match the new opening. Working in harmony with the top chop, the car was lowered 3 inches at each end.

To accentuate the long, sweeping lines, Sam extended the rear fenders 4 inches and added taillights from a '53 Pontiac station wagon. In the front the stock headlights were set aside in favor of

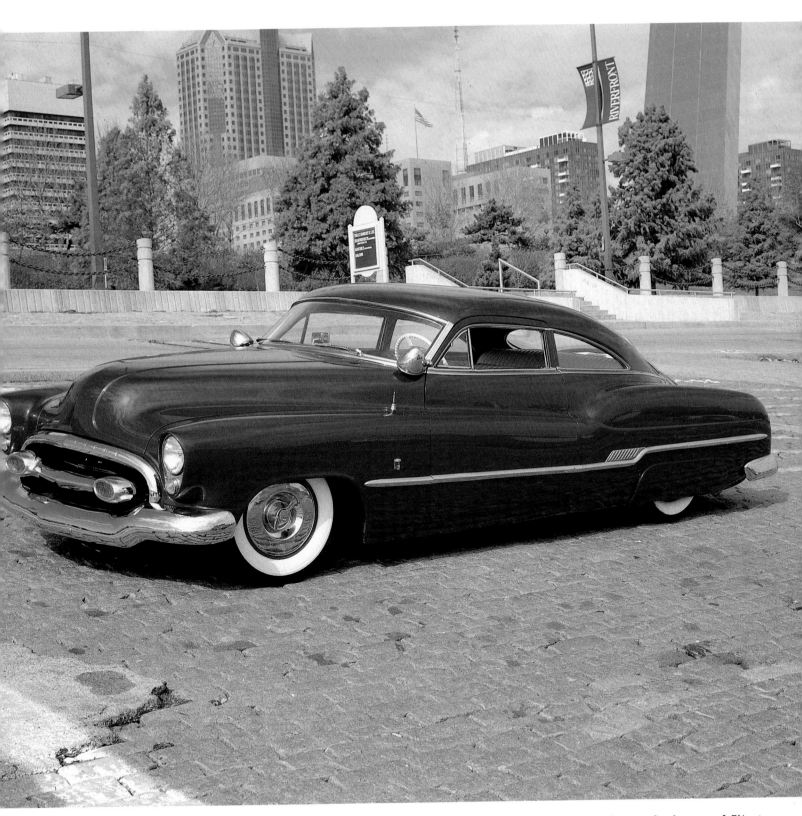

The Sam Barris Buick displays the sleek, clean look that the brothers were known for. Like many of their cars, Sam's Buick has a chopped top—3½ inches at the front and 5½ at the rear—to provide the proper tapering line.

Seen along the old river front in St. Louis, the Buick carries side trim from a '54 Lincoln, a Barris crest on the front fender and hand-formed fender skirts.

Rear taillight, opposite, is from a '53 Pontiac station wagon, maroon paint is the same color Sam used in 1953. Parts like these taillights were difficult to find when the car was restored.

Long, low look of Sam's Buick seems much in contrast with the tall, thin St. Louis arch.

The plan for the Buick was both modest and grand

As the car started to come together there were all the little details to attend to, like the door handles that disappeared in favor of electric solenoids and the side trim from a '51 Lincoln, turned upside down. The hubcaps are from a '53 Caddy with knock-offs added. The fender skirts were Sam's own, formed by hand.

As the car neared completion Sam chose a maroon and white interior, stitched up by the Carson Top Shop.

It took twenty-two months, working part time, to finish the Buick. Magazines from the period were impressed by both the quality and quantity of the work. In fact, the February 1954 issue of *Rod & Custom* reported that "had the car been built for a customer the bill would have been a staggering $2,400 with the top chopping alone accounting for $800."

The story of the Buick started with the end of the war. In a similar fashion, the story goes on well past its completion in late 1953. Sam enjoyed his new custom and drove it extensively, but the enjoyment was short-lived. In 1954 Sam's son, John, was having trouble with his eyes. Correction could be done by surgery; the surgery would be very expensive.

It helps to remember that this was before the days of Blue Cross or Major Medical plans. When Sam heard what the operation was going to cost he realized there was only one answer.

After the Buick was sold, the historical record gets a little cloudy. Somehow the car passed from hand to hand until it passed into the possession of a drag racer. In the early 1960s the beautiful Buick was often seen campaigning in the northeastern states. In place of the straight-eight, a wild, Nail-Head Buick V-8 was installed. Sam's careful work inside the trunk was cut aside so tubs and massive rear tires could be fitted.

Later in the 1960s the Buick was missing again. It hadn't been seen for some time, not on the drag strip, not anywhere. It finally surfaced in about 1975 at the Hershey, Pennsylvania, swap meet. Jim Walker, long-time admirer of Barris customs, came upon a derelict old Buick body with no engine and no transmission. On the hood of this heap were written the words "Sam Barris '50 Buick." Jim remembered the original Buick; it didn't seem possible that this refugee from the

new assemblies from a '53 Buick, Frenched into the front fenders. If the front end seems to have a little Oldsmobile about it, it's probably because the center grille is borrowed from a '53 Olds. The bumper itself is from a '53 Lincoln.

When Sam cut the top he used the original rear window, mounted at a new lower angle. The top of the trunk was dropped 5 inches to meet the new lower line of the top.

Interior follows standard 1950s themes. Large steering wheel is stock, as is the heavy chrome on the dash. Seats are done in maroon with contrasting buttons flanked by maroon and white door panels.

Let us hope that in another forty years people will still care about the dreams and creations of their forebears to preserve and display an especially stylish old Buick

crusher was the same car featured on the cover of *Rod & Custom* in 1954. The top was caved in, the glass was gone, there was no body trim, no bumpers—the car was just a body, just barely.

The Barris Buick, if it could still be called that, belonged to Leo Gephart. Jim Walker and Leo are both from Dayton, Ohio, and they're both in the car business. Jim discussed the car with Leo—could it be restored, was it possible to undo the years of neglect? Jim finally decided that restoring the car was impossible and the Buick went back to Dayton with Leo.

Jim couldn't get the Buick out of his head, however. Every time he saw Leo on other business, the Buick somehow came into the conversation. Finally it was too much; Jim offered Leo a swap and brought the Buick home.

The first step, a new drivetrain, was accomplished when Jim found a '50 Riviera two-door in good condition. The Barris body was set down on the new/old chassis and the serious restoration work could begin.

Dave Oakes did most of the work, repairing the roof and body panels, and reinstalling the glass. He and Jim read all the old magazines they could find and then went shopping for Lincoln trim and Oldsmobile grille sections.

Finally the car was finished and looked every bit as wonderful as it did in 1954. George Barris saw the Buick at a show in Indianapolis in about 1981 and gave it his personal seal of approval. After enjoying the car for a number of years and displaying it at some KKOA events, Jim sold the Buick to Kurt McCormick, the Buick's current owner.

Another big fan of Barris customs, Kurt parked the Buick next to a '55 Chevrolet built by George Barris in the late 1950s. Since buying the car, Kurt has done some mechanical repairs but mostly he just enjoys the car. There are KKOA shows to attend, pesky photographers to accommodate and that occasional Sunday drive.

Headlight assemblies are from a '53 Buick, a new car at the time Sam built his custom.

The Sam Barris Buick was built almost forty years ago by a gifted craftsman. Over the years the car has been saved and restored by other men out of respect for the talents and genius of Sam and brother George. Let us hope that in another forty years people still care enough about the dreams and creations of their forebears to preserve and display an especially stylish old Buick.

Dream Truck

Capturing the dreams of a generation

Among the well-known cars from the early days of customizing there is one that stands out as better known and better viewed than any other. The vehicle in question was a project for a certain well-known magazine. And while nearly every automotive magazine has produced features on their own project vehicle, this one project vehicle worked better—for readers and publishers alike—than any other.

The vehicle in question is the *Rod & Custom* magazine *Dream Truck*. Never before have so many enthusiasts participated in the design and building of a vehicle. And never before (or since?) has a magazine done such a wonderful job of following the progress of a project vehicle, writing some great tech and how-to stories in the process. Rather than simply describing

the *Dream Truck* and all the modifications that were made, it might be more instructive to follow the construction of the truck as described in thirty-two issues of *Rod & Custom* magazine.

The series of articles defining and explaining the *Dream Truck* started in the September 1953 issue. The topic of that first story was an engine swap—all the rage in 1953—more specifically an Oldsmobile Rocket V–8 set into a '41 Chevrolet frame. It seems the idea of the *Dream Truck* evolved from that first tech story. As of the first installment there was no truck and no master plan to follow a project vehicle through various stages of customizing. The editors knew only that there were thousands of young men out there with a powerful thirst for automotive knowledge, and that keeping them as readers meant satisfying that thirst.

By the time the next installment appeared in May 1954 there was a truck cab, and the project was referred to as *R & C's* "rolling laboratory." The article was titled, "Top Chopping—The Right Way." The work was performed by well-known body man and customizer Sam Gates. The photos (and presumably the writing as well) were done by the editor, Spencer Murray. Spence set a pattern for later how-to stories by breaking the top chop into two thorough articles.

Part II of the top chop appeared in the June 1954 issue. Like Part I, the article was well done and well illustrated—the material could still be used today as a good how-to story. Excerpts are useful both for tone and to show where the project was heading:

"The cab belongs to *R & C* and its readers, and as such is to receive whatever suggestions you might suggest. Immediately after the top job is concluded, the cab will be mounted on a Chevy chassis equipped with an Oldsmobile V8 engine coupled to a Hydra-Matic transmission. . . . Articles dealing with alteration to the car will be generalized upon so that readers can apply such modifications to their particular cars, regardless of body style. We feel that this will be the answer for those who have written to us requesting specific customizing information on this or that, but

Dream Truck *exhibits a number of features, each built by a separate custom shop. Considering all the people who had a hand in its construction, the design of the Dream Truck works surprisingly well. On the next pages, the* combination of the 3½ inch top chop and 5 inch sectioning job creates a low, sleek custom with little resemblance to a stock '54 Chevy pickup.

the answer to which we have been unable to give them—until now."

Part II of the top chopping story covered more than just the top chop. Included in the article was a good description of an almost lost art, hammer-welding. The description began with an admonishment to those who use too much lead:

"This business of using lead as a quick way of completing a job is strictly for the birds. By way of proof, Sam began the finish metal work on the top insert. The project was started by grinding off the burned paint and scale . . . then, much to our surprise, he put the grinder away stating it would not be used again. . . . But there before our eyes, Sam finished off the top with nothing more than a hammer, a dolly, the torch and a file. . . . Using the torch Sam heated an inch long section of the weld to a hot cherry red. Then, quickly putting the torch aside before the metal cooled appreciably, he took up his hammer and dolly and swiftly pounded the small area. The welded ridge became flattened, thus conforming to the surrounding metal, and the adjoining pieces of metal and the weld itself became united as a single, flat section with no visible break or line. . . ."

In the last paragraph Spence reminds his readers to send in "your suggestions for without them we will have no idea what you want your pickup truck to look like."

The job of customizing the *Dream Truck* was performed by a variety of shops. The job of building a new dash—August 1954 issue—was handled by Clay Jensen and Neil Emory at Valley Custom. The first photograph shows an air chisel blade being run along the top of the stock dash. Because the new design called for a gauge cluster in the center of the dash, an oval ring was formed from steel bar stock and tack-welded in place. Next, the two rolled sides of the dash were formed from sheet stock and tack-welded on either side of the large oval ring. Step by step, the new dash took shape until Neil and Clay had created a clean, rolled shape that ran from side to side with an oval in the center for the speedo and tachometer.

Not content with a top 3 inches lower than stock and no doubt in search of more articles, the *R & C*

Dream Truck was taken back to Sam Gates' shop so 5 inches could be sectioned out of the middle. Following the earlier example, this story was broken down into two parts. Part I, September 1954, was spent explaining all the planing necessary for a successful sectioning job. Spence went to great lengths to explain where the metal should be cut (at the widest point in the body), how it should be cut (neatly) and the importance of the inner body structure.

Between Part I and Part II of the sectioning story Sam Gates' shop got busy so the *R & C* rolling laboratory rolled to Valley Custom in Burbank, California. Owners Neil and Clay (builders of the dash) were contracted to finish the sectioning job. Most of the long strips of metal had been removed from the doors and body panels. It remained for Clay and Neil to cut through the corners and door openings, always left for last, and accomplish what Spence called the "Great Drop."

Special care was taken in the area of the cowl and door hinges. The 5 inch cut through the body was done above the fender line, though the boys were careful not to cut through the original mounting holes for the hood hinges. After the drop the body halves were welded back together, starting at the door openings. All finish work was done with more hammer-welding and a minimum of the dreaded lead.

Near the end of the story the differences between a file and a grinder were pointed out: "A body grinder, fitted with a #16 disc, was run back and forth over the general area (where the two body halves had been welded together). . . . The grinder was not used to smooth the metal prior to painting! The edge of a grinder disc is very flexible so had a tendency to drip into the unseen valley. . . ." Instead, warns Valley Custom Shop, a Vixen body file should be used. This is a long, flat, cross-tooth file especially made for filing sheet metal. "As it is drawn back and forth across the metal, the high spots become outstanding from the surrounding metal due to the cutting action of the file's teeth. The low spots are then tapped from behind with a pick hammer to elevate them to the same extent as the higher areas. . . . Continuing in the above manner, all of the welded seams of the *R & C* pickup truck disappeared and became bright, shiny steel."

Someplace between the October 1954 and the July 1955 issue someone realized that the much modified '54 Chevy truck cab would not transfer easily to the '41 Chevy chassis. In the July issue, Spence explained that the coupe chassis had been discarded in favor of a complete, clean '50 Chevrolet half-ton

Rear grille opening and grille were built by George Barris. Fins were the first "annual change" and were built by Bob Metz.

pickup truck. The rest of the issue went on to describe the advantages of the new dropped front axle, from Bell Axle company. On page 83 an ad for the Auto Discount Company lists their specials for the month: White sidewall kits for $9.95 or Super Deluxe Flare Fender Skirts starting at $11.95.

The August 1955 issue gave readers a series of how-to's based on the rolling laboratory. There were wheels to reverse, tonneau covers to build (called a tarpaulin back then), gravel shields to install, tailgates to smooth and '39 Chevrolet taillights to install in the

rear fenders. At the end of the light installation it was explained that "this simple installation alone brought about a great appearance change in *R & C*'s ½ ton, and suffice it to say that the $5.50 spent for the lights (new) was money well spent."

The *Dream Truck*'s place in history was ensured with the publication of the October 1955 issue. The *Dream Truck* became the first car (or truck) to get the new 265 ci Chevy Turbofire V-8 as a transplanted motor. Apparently, someone with the magazine had a connection at GM. The small-block that went into the

Front grille opening was formed from two Studebaker front pans, joined and modified to form an oval. Grille was built of bar stock and tubing. Turn and parking lights were built into the ends of the tubing.

Dream Truck was the first of millions that would be transplanted in years to come.

Spence and the boys lucked out on the first small-block motor swap. When they tried to mate the truck's three-speed tranny to the V-8's clutch and bellhousing, everything slid together like it was meant to be. They discovered later that the pre 1954 car transmissions used a different and noncompatible bolt pattern. The balance of Part II, "Out With The Old," gives readers the options for mating 6 and 12 volt systems, hooking up the shift linkage and connecting the oil pressure gauge. In conclusion, Spence reports: "It's been fun. The pickup goes like a scalded cat and

after a brief interlude of a month or so we'll be back with a factual report on acceleration, etc. . . ."

When the chopped and sectioned cab was placed on the new/old pickup chassis (the one they put the V-8 into), the boys from *R & C* decided to go in for some other modifications as well. Under the heading "What Happened to the Front End" the copy reads: "As careful perusers of the accompanying text may have noted, we dropped the truck 5 inches by what was blithely referred to as a 'relatively simple project.' Just what was meant is now to be revealed. . . . It is immediately obvious that something must be done to the springs in order to achieve the quest for less-than-stock height. The answer lies in relocating the springs below the axle. The amount of drop available through this manner can be determined in inches. . . ."

The rear of the truck was dropped by using 4 inch lowering blocks. That was determined to be insufficient so the spring perch brackets were modified to lower the rear another 4 inches. When the sectioned cab was mounted to the chassis with the stock box, the height of the box made the cab look squashed. The solution was channeling the box to ride lower on the frame. Keeping the truck looking right was accomplished by raising the fenders on the sides of the box the same amount the box was lowered.

More than three years after starting the series, *R & C* started a series within a series called "Barris Meets the Truck." The first of this mini-series (it is a small truck) describes the initial reworking of the front end of the *Dream Truck*. The grille opening was formed by using two Studebaker lower grille sections put together to form an oval.

The January 1957 issue details the finishing of the grille project. First the forward edge of the hood is trimmed. Finishing the edges where the new grille shell meets the fenders is done with lead. The captions for the illustrations (photos by George Barris) provided some insights to the fine art of lead working: "Lead won't stick to bare metal, so tinning compound is applied by heating steel wool and dipping into compound. Steel wool is next brushed over seams after metal has been heated, until shiny surface appears. Lead goes on right after tinning. Here the stick is shown being heated until it becomes semi-fluid. Practice playing torch back and forth from metal to lead will make the operation become automatic, make leading easier. . . . Once lead adheres to metal, it must be reheated and worked into approximate contour with wooden paddle . . . paddles must be dipped in beeswax to prevent lead sticking to wooden surface. . . ."

The February 1957 issue, Part III of the Barris series, covered the conversion to quad headlights. The idea of using quads had been suggested three years earlier in sketches by the *R & C* stylist Lynn Wineland. The article was a series of twenty-two photographs with captions. The photos began with the creation of two, figure-eight shaped metal outlines. The outlines became the basis for the new quad system. George and the boys did major surgery on the front fenders, each step carefully explained with a lengthy caption. Eventually, expanded metal was mounted inside the figure eight, and the housings for the lights mounted to the expanded metal.

Part IV, "Barris Meets the Truck," covered the creation of the nicely sculptured hood scoop. The "dished" section and the scoop itself were created on an English wheel by race car builder Jack Sutton. The new scoop was designed to deliver fresh air to both the cab and the engine compartment.

The final installment of the Barris series dealt with the creation of the grille. The decision was made to create an entirely new grille using bar stock and exhaust tubing. Readers were admonished to follow *R & C*'s lead and "take the build-it-yourself grille route instead of trying to adapt an existing unit into a hole which was not intended for it."

The two large diameter tubes were bent in the middle after hacksawing a small notch, and trimmed to length. The Lucite lenses on the ends were built by Bob Hirohata and attached with small screws from behind. The smaller bars were simply bar stock, heated and bent to fit and then sent out to the chrome shop. Perhaps the most significant thing about the grille was the approach rather than the design itself. Rather than buying or adapting a grille, *R & C* chose to make one using a very pragmatic approach—use what you got and let's try to be original.

The balance of the articles, except for the last one, were a wrapup of the project and include coverage of the first shows the *Dream Truck* attended. While the last of the how-to articles ran into mid 1957, the truck was finished and on display at some eastern car shows early in that same year.

The project was intended to represent the cutting edge of customizing. Rather than creating a vehicle that would withstand the test of time, the *Dream Truck* was intended to change as the years went by. The first annual change, as they were called, was performed by Bob Metz at his shop in Shelbyville, Indiana. A well-known customizer, Bob created the fins and the rear quarter panels, taking the truck from customized step-side to more radical custom. The rear grille work is the work of George Barris, done at the same time as the front grille. Bob Metz chose to blend the earlier Barris work with his own.

From Indiana the *Dream Truck* went to Hawaii

for the First Annual Hawaiian Motorama. The October 1957 issue carried a picture of the truck, with fins, on the boat ready to unload at Honolulu.

After Honolulu there were more shows and more road miles. By October 1958 more than one million enthusiasts are believed to have seen the truck at the various shows. And it was on the way to another show, this one in Des Moines, Iowa, that the truck met with disaster.

The January 1959 issue of *Rod & Custom* carried a sad, two-page obituary to the long and glorious *Dream Truck* series. The pictures showed a beautiful truck on its side in a ditch in Kansas. The copy spoke of an uncertain future and the promise of another Dream Project. Spence ended his farewell address with these words: "Our thanks to all who took part in the unfortunate truck's construction . . . and to the countless thousands who watched the truck grow from an idea born some five years ago into reality. . . . And so, Dream Truck, you certainly served your purpose—that of showing doubting Thomases the country over just what this business of hot rodding and customizing is all about."

That epitaph was not the end of the *Dream Truck.* It turns out that *Dream Truck* was an appropriate name for the vehicle because it encompassed the dreams of a generation of young men—dreams that refused to die. After twenty years in limbo the truck started the long road back to restoration. Against great odds and sound advice, the truck has been returned to its original 1957 condition.

Today the truck belongs to Kurt McCormick of St. Louis, Missouri. Kurt has finished repairs to the front suspension, the last of the repairs necessary for the truck's complete restoration. A final end to a project that was started some thirty-seven years earlier.

Dream Truck *was one of the first to use quad lights, beating other customs as well as Detroit to the new headlight system.*

A Re-Creation

The best of the 1950s in a 1980s car

The custom movement can be divided into two periods: the heydays of the 1950s through the early 1960s, and the rebirth which started in the early 1980s.

The cars from chapters two and three represent those early days when life was good and customs lined the curbs of mainstreet America. The cars in the later chapters, however, have all been built during the renaissance of customizing—the early to late 1980s.

There is one car ideally suited to act as the transition vehicle—the one vehicle that ties the two periods together. That vehicle is pictured here, a car built in 1985 to represent the best of the early 1950s.

In 1953 the already famous Barris brothers became more famous with the unveiling of their newest creation, a '51 Mercury built for Bob Hirohata (pronounced Hero-ata). To say the car was a hit is an understatement. The March 1953 issues of *Hop Up* and *Motor Trend* featured the Merc on the cover, while *Hot Rod* carried a feature inside. In months to

come, the small magazines would run features on the car as well. The Hirohata Merc became a benchmark, the car young men dreamed of owning and customizers dreamed of building.

Despite the acclaim, the trophies and the car's role in a major movie, the Merc was sold and sold again until by 1959 it was on the back row of a used car lot. Eventually the Merc disappeared. By the mid 1980s, when the custom movement was in the high gear of nostalgia, the famous Merc hadn't been seen for so long it was assumed gone for good. Some said it had been cut up. Others said its whereabouts were known by a select few but the current owner would not cooperate with any plans to sell or restore it.

At about the same time, two men in Kansas City were having a series of conversations that would bring about a re-creation of the famous Mercury. Jack Walker, owner of a number of fine customs, was spending a lot of time in the shop of Doug Thompson, master customizer and builder. They were finishing up restoration work on another car when Jack commented, "You know Doug, I think the next car I want you to build will have to be a '50 or '51 Merc."

When Jack Walker said '51 Merc, it set wheels turning in Doug Thompson's head. Doug was sixteen when the Hirohata car made its debut in 1953. That one car had an impact on him like no other. Even today Doug still remembers the car's appearance: "You have to understand, Sam and George Barris were really why I had become a customizer. When I saw the original Hirohata Merc in the magazines in 1953, I swore that someday I would be that good—good enough to build a car like that."

One thing led to another and in 1983 Jack Walker showed up at Doug's shop with a nice clean '51 Merc club coupe. By this time they had agreed that the car to be built would be more than just another chopped Merc—it would be a re-creation of *the* chopped Merc. The one Mercury that everyone's been copying ever since.

They knew the project would be a lot of work. What they didn't know was just how much.

Though built in 1985 by Doug Thompson, the lines and dimensions of this Merc match exactly the dimensions of the original Hirohata car, built in 1953 by the Barris brothers. On the next pages, another example of the Barris look, the Hirohata Merc seems to fall away toward the rear. Effect is created by chopping the top more in the rear. Buick side spear and Lincoln taillights heighten the effect.

Doug Thompson: "You have to understand, Sam and George Barris were really why I had become a customizer"

The first problem was where to start. The original car was not available to provide measurements, there were no blueprints and the original builder, Sam Barris, was dead. They were forced to start with the magazines.

Based solely on the copy and photographs in *Hop Up, Motor Trend* and the others, Doug started into the cutting and reshaping of the Mercury. In order to create the right shape to duplicate the Barris look, Doug started with, and took great pains in, chopping the top.

At the front the top was cut 4 inches while at the rear 7 inches were removed. As Sam probably did so many years before, Doug cut the rear window from the top with its surrounding metalwork, with plans to reinstall it later at a new angle.

One of the things that set the Hirohata apart from other customs of the period was the side window treatment. Instead of just cutting the window opening in the door to match the new top, Sam and George chose to eliminate the center post altogether. In order to duplicate that hardtop effect, Doug had to fabricate some channel (none of the correct dimensions could be found), heat and bend it to shape and then send it out to the chrome shop.

As the new top came together, the original rear window was reinstalled in its new position. Next, the gently curving, chrome window trim was installed in the doors. While Doug was working away in the shop, his parts runner was calling and chasing all over the country looking for an odd assortment of old parts.

The agreement between Doug and Jack specified that Doug do the actual work while Jack was responsible for finding the necessary parts. Necessary parts included arcane pieces like '49 Caddy hubcaps, '52 Buick side trim, '52 Lincoln taillights, a '51 Ford grille and a special steering wheel offered as an option on some '50 and '51 Merc convertibles.

After reinstalling the top, Doug turned his attention to the rear fenders. The original car featured functional scoops ahead of the rear wheels, flush fit fender skirts and Frenched taillight lenses. Re-creating those features and duplicating the original lines proved a test of Doug's patience.

It took four tries, but finally the rear quarter panel matched the lines of the original. As Doug and Jack weathered the difficult parts of the project, there seemed to be an unspoken agreement—the Merc would match the original as closely as was humanly possible. Whenever one man would waver or doubt their ability to finish the project, the other would gently remind the offender that they were in this together, that nothing less than perfection would be accepted.

After correctly finishing one rear quarter panel, the measurements could be transferred to the other side. Next, the Lincoln taillights were Frenched into the fenders and an antenna mounted in each fender. To duplicate the rear bumper, exhaust ports were created from oval pipe.

The next major snag came after the headlights were Frenched into the front fenders. Doug reports Frenching the headlights in standard custom fashion and the shock that came afterward: "I had used '52 Ford headlight rings to set the headlights into the fender. Everything was just fine until I got both sides roughed in and stepped back across the shop to have a good look. The more I looked the more obvious it became—the original car had fenders that were longer than ours. But there was nothing in any of the articles about extending the fenders. . . ."

Doug was having doubts again but this time it was his daughter, a commercial artist, who helped him see the light. She simply took a caliper and a proportion wheel to the picture of the original and then transferred those measurements to the car in the shop. Because the doors were the same length on both cars, she was able to compare the door dimensions to the fender length of both Mercurys.

"After looking at her measurements it became obvious that Sam Barris had extended the entire fender forward in addition to Frenching the headlight," Doug says. "It was like the problem with the rear quarters; we weren't just creating a car we thought looked good, we were recreating a car from a set of photographs—which turned out to be much more difficult."

The Barris brothers had created one more little puzzle for Jack and Doug—how had the large, single bar grille been created? By the time Doug had solved the puzzle he had also gained some insight into the methods used by the brothers Barris. The grille was made from a '51 Ford grille, the bullets were removed and the outside pieces were moved in. Doug explains: "They made the grille the same way they made most of

Note the hardtop, created by cutting away the window post and replacing it with chrome channel. Rear window is from stock top, mounted at a new, more horizontal angle.

their cars—with a real straightforward, simple approach. They took materials that were readily available and made them work."

After finishing the front sheet metal there were a thousand small details to take care of, things like

mounting the Buick side trim and getting the car ready for paint. Before putting paint on the Merc Doug followed standard 1950s practice in getting the car as low as possible. In the front the coils were cut, and the spindles heated and reshaped to compensate

43

for any camber change. In the rear the springs were flattened and lowering blocks were installed.

Because the driveshaft sat higher now relative to the body, the center of the floor was removed and a new tunnel constructed. The interior work was turned over to Bob Sipes from Grandview, Missouri. Without any good detail shots of the interior, Doug and Jack gave Bob directions as best they could. Shortly after Bob finished the new stitching, Kurt McCormick (owner of four Barris cars and much memorabilia) supplied pictures of the Merc's interior taken in 1953 or 1954. With the pictures in hand Jack took the car back to Bob Sipes so the interior could be done correctly.

The question of authenticity raised its head again when Doug and Jack considered the powerplant. The original car had a Cadillac motor mated to the Mercury three-speed overdrive transmission. Jack was reluctant to install a Caddy engine and further erode the budget. It was one of those occasions when Doug gave a gentle nudge, reminding Jack of their commitment.

Bob Peterson rebuilt and installed the Cadillac engine. Kurt McCormick came through again with a genuine Hellings air bonnet to sit on top of the Rochester carb.

Finally Doug could apply the paint, a light seafoam green above the Buick chrome spear and dark organic green below it. After painting there was a race against time to clean up the Merc, finish the little details and get it to the Lead Sled Nationals in Springfield, Ohio.

Few people knew about the car ahead of time. When Jack drove in he created quite a stir. All weekend long the car was the focus of attention with people wanting to know if this was the original or what.

Later that year Jack's Mercury took the George Barris Best Custom award at the Rod Powell show in Monterey, California. In fact, the car was so well

Interior colors match those of the exterior. Laminated knobs were all the rage in '53—the originals were built by Bob Hirohata; these were built by Jack Walker.

Just like the original car, rear fender is ventilated with a scoop and three small chrome teeth used as accents.

received at the Rod Powell show that Jack and Doug were invited to bring the car to the invitation-only Oakland Roadster show. By the time that first show season was over the Merc had captured both the George Barris Best Custom and Sam Barris Memorial awards.

Since that heady first season the car has been featured in a number of magazines, including the European press. Demand remains constant, including a showing at the 1989 Street Rod Nationals in St. Paul, Minnesota, where the Mercury appeared in the Top Flight booth.

Doug and Jack have built more than a great car, more than the re-creation of a special custom. They have built a transition vehicle, one that stands as a reminder that the custom movement we enjoy today owes a large debt to the pioneers who came before.

Pro-Custom

A football player turned ballerina

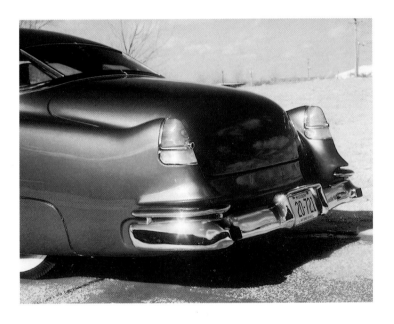

When Larry Cochran bought the '50 Chevy seen here his intention was to build a mean, pro-street Chevy. An aggressive, nitrous oxide kind of machine with massive rear tires and unlimited horsepower. What he ended up with instead is one of the most beautiful customs seen in a long, long time. The story of the Chevy's evolution from pro-street to pro-custom involves Doug Thompson and a friend Larry and Doug have in common: Jack Walker.

It all started in the fall of 1984 as Doug and Jack Walker worked on the re-creation of the Hirohata Mercury. One day Jack explained that he would be temporarily unable to continue the project, because of a certain cash shortfall. The real problem, though, went deeper than that.

Doug Thompson has a waiting list of customers, men with custom projects waiting for Doug's time the way people take numbers while they wait at the

butcher shop. Because of this list, Doug has a rule: If a customer pulls a car out of the shop before it's finished it goes to the back of the line. Jack's problem was how to get the Merc out of the shop for a few months without going to the back of the line. When Larry talked to Jack about wanting the top chopped on a recently acquired '50 Chevy, Jack could see a way out of his dilemma.

Jack suggested to Doug that he take in the Chevy top chop as part of the Mercury project, and promised that he would bring the Merc back in as soon as Doug was finished.

In late 1984 Doug chopped the top on Larry's Chevy: 4 inches in the front and 5 inches in the rear. Simple, nothing to it—except for the three-piece rear window. With the top cut the small, triangular-shaped side windows wouldn't fit no matter what. New ones were finally made out of plexiglass.

The front window was changed at the same time. A one-piece 1950 Olds windshield was cut and installed for its more modern looks. Because of the top chop, the angle of the new windshield became a little steeper than before.

Before the car left the shop the front wheel openings were radiused. This last bit of work was done, as Doug describes, "against my better judgment, because we didn't have a total concept yet." Once the fender work was done Larry picked up the Chevy and Doug thought that was the last time he'd see the car.

Somehow, in the time it took to finish Jack's Mercury, Larry had a change of heart. Oh, he did have a Chevrolet 350 engine installed complete with Nova subframe. And he had the Nova rear end installed in place of the stock Chevy piece. But the 350 motor was left nearly stock and the plans for giant rear tires were put on the shelf.

Instead of the pro-street Larry decided that the car would be a custom. Larry also decided the man to finish the work should be the same man who started it.

When the car came back into Doug's shop the first decision to be made involved the front sheet metal.

Sometimes known as a Chevillac, this '50 Chevrolet carries rear taillight assemblies from a Cadillac. Front fenders have been extended 2 inches; front grille is originally from a Chrysler Imperial.

Strong, sculptured line along the side makes the Chevy seem longer than it really is. Scoops in rear fenders are functional, directing cooling air to rear brakes. Lakes pipes have been molded into the rocker panel.

The problem was tire clearance in a turn—the combination of lowering and the wider stance of the Nova subframe meant the front tires rubbed whenever the wheels were turned.

Larry asked Doug what he thought they ought to do. Doug grabbed a panel cutter and quickly removed 4 inches all the way around the fender lip—the same fender lip that had been radiused earlier. When the color returned to Larry's face he wanted to know what was going on? Doug explained later: "When I've got a problem I believe in getting the problem out of the way and then moving ahead. We now had the clearance we needed. What was next?"

The fender flares were the answer to the question. After deciding to flare the fender lips, Doug suggested a sculptured line running from the flare to the rear of the car. Once the fender flare and horizontal line were decided upon, the rest of the car just kind of fell into place. Running the sculptured metal along the side of the body created a strong, horizontal line, making the car seem longer than it really is. To enhance that long, low look Doug extended the front headlight rim 2 inches and then Frenched the lights.

Finishing out the front end is a variety of parts chosen with the greatest care. The grille shell is from a '50 Mercury, molded into the Chevrolet front sheet metal. The grille itself is from a '59 Imperial, though many think it came from a '54 Chevy. The finished grille was formed from the center of the Imperial grille mated to bumper guards from a '51 Mercury. The parking and turn lights are mounted in small housings behind the toothy, Imperial grille.

The front bumper is from a '50 Chevrolet, California edition. California law required that bumpers be one piece, and customizers have long preferred these for their cleaner lines. But before the bumper could be mounted on the custom there were a few modifications. First, the license plate frame was added along with the horizontal trim pieces at the corners. Next, brackets were built behind the bumper so none of the mounting bolts would show. Finally, the new frame and trim were molded into the bumper (without the benefit of Bondo) so there would be no seams.

Larry and Doug decided on some serious hood louvers, but first they decided to modify the hood. The original '50 Chevy used a two-part affair riveted in the center. Wanting to keep the car as clean and seam-free as possible, Doug hammer-welded the two halves together eliminating any seam. He then ventilated the hood with 150 louvers.

The doors were treated to the same sculptured line that originates at the front fender lip. To create the line across the door, Doug had sheet metal bent on a sheet metal brake and then welded it to the door skin. Once the line was created in the door skin, there was the problem of making sure the door crease would clear the edge of the fender when the door opened.

The sculptured line running across the door becomes the upper edge of the functional scoop built into the forward edge of the rear fender. Scoops have been used since the first customs were built as a styling accent. What no one remembers is that scoops started out with a functional rather than a styling purpose. Larry's Chevrolet, a car with skirts sitting 2 inches off the ground, doesn't get much air to the rear brakes. The scoops were the answer to a problem. The

Master craftsman Doug Thompson, a customizer for over thirty years. Doug built Larry's Chevillac as well as the Hirohata Merc re-creation. On the next pages, upper panels are covered with Candy Root Beer, lowers with Candy Apricot. Instead of using chrome trim to separate the two colors, Doug Thompson used the sculptured line along the side as the color break.

Freezing rain the night before provides the sparkling background. Low-riding stance is created by lowering the car almost 7 inches and taking more than 4 inches out of the roof.

three chrome nuggets are the styling accent, as if to say, Look here, this scoop has a job to do.

Below the door, running along the rocker panel is another traditional custom feature, the Lakes pipes. In this case the pipes emerge from the lower fender and run along the much modified rocker panel, providing both a nice 1950s touch and a chrome accent along the bottom of the car.

The skirts used to fill the rear fender opening are stock pieces modified so the lower edge runs along the bottom of the rear fender. The fender itself is also Chevrolet; some people think the whole fender or at least the rear quarter panel has been lifted from a Cadillac. The '53 Caddy donated only the taillight assembly and 12 inches of metal extending from the light.

The Cadillac light was used to clean up the lines of the stock Chevrolet. On the street the Chevy was known as a "bustleback" in reference to the hump in the trunk lid. While the trunk lid had a hump, the fenders had a smoothly tapering line that ran to the bumper without as much as a hiccup. Doug used the Caddy light assembly to introduce a hump to the rear fender line, similar to the hump in the trunk lid.

To protect those light assemblies a '52 Pontiac rear bumper was used complete with the same small, horizontal trim pieces used on the front. Doug used heavy wall, 2 x 4 inch pipe to make the exhaust outlets and like the front bumper, all the seams have been eliminated with careful metal finishing.

Once the body work was finished there was the interior to take care of. Working along traditional lines, the dashboard with all its wonderful chrome brackets and bezels was left nearly stock. The factory radio was disassembled and modified so a push on the buttons operates things like door solenoids and the power antenna. The real radio is mounted in the glove box. Below the dash a Vintage Air heating and cooling

unit keeps everything comfortable. The interior stitching was performed by Bob Sipes in a brown velour, pleated and rolled.

The finished Chevrolet is a long way from Larry's original street machine concept. Instead of racing, this Chevy's built to cruise. Instead of being an aggressive machine, the Chevrolet is a graceful beauty. Larry started out wanting a big, mean, football player kind of a car, shoulder pads and all. What he got instead is the queen of the prom—in a slinky new dress.

Front bumper is from a '50 Chevy, California edition without seams. Brackets on the rear of the bumper hide those unsightly bolts. Imperial grille rides in '50 Mercury grille shell.

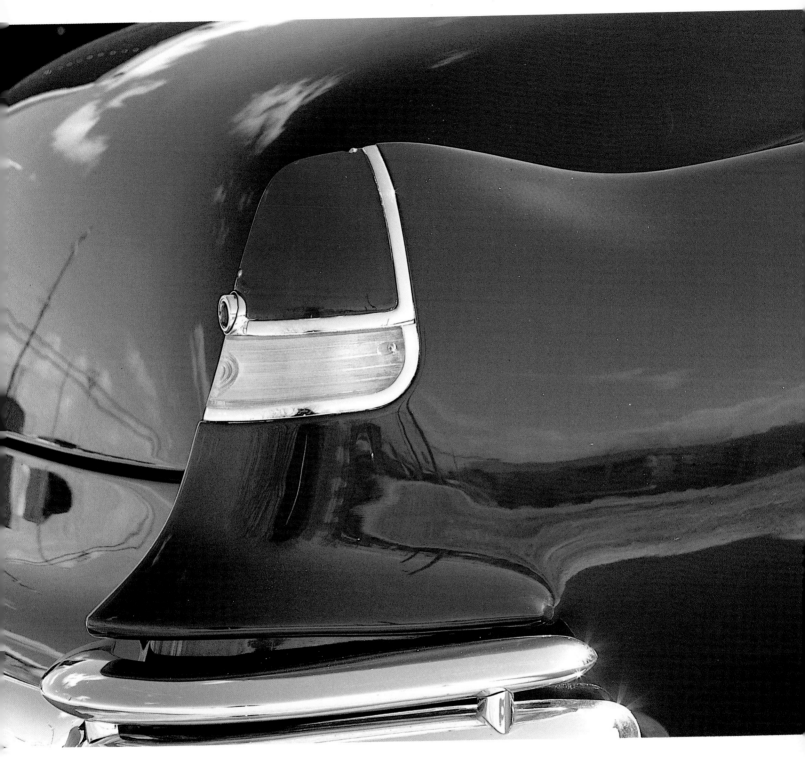

*Light assemblies are from a '53 Cadillac, grafted to the
original fenders with the greatest of care.*

Plum Wild Buick

Skill, teamwork and dedication— united we stand

One of the most popular customs built recently is the '51 Buick of Ray and Myrna Bozarth of West Liberty, Iowa. Designed by M. K. Johns, built by Merlin Berg and upholstered by Jim McFall—with lots of ideas and inspiration from both Ray and Myrna—the car took just more than one year to build. Like some of the most popular and legendary cars from the 1950s, the Buick seems to have a special magic—a design where everything turned out just right.

It was during the Buick's first outing, at the Lead Sled Spectacular in 1988, that Ray and Myrna got

some inkling of what they had created. Their Buick, finished only three days earlier, took home both the coveted Bradley award as well as Koolest Wild Kemp. As the summer continued, so did the awards: Best Radical Custom at the James Dean run, Koolest Kemp at Last Pass, and Best of Show at the Mid-State Nationals.

Encouraged by the early awards and with support from their many friends, Ray and Myrna decided to take their custom to the big time: the Oakland Roadster show. Wondering if they were stepping out of their league, Ray and Myrna soldiered across the mountains with the Buick in tow.

When the dust settled on the West Coast, the beautiful plum Buick had taken no less than five awards: Outstanding Engineered, Best Hand Built Custom, Outstanding in Class, Best Paint and Best Interior. At the Sacramento Autorama the Buick did a repeat, taking home the same five trophies plus the Sam Barris Memorial award.

Summer number two was more of the same with no letup in sight. As the Buick enters its third summer, requests for the car are still coming in strong.

One is tempted to ask, How? How did this group of people create such a popular car? Why did it work for the Buick and not the Merc or the Chevy or the blue Ford or . . .

In the beginning there was a sketch. Ray commissioned M. K. "Kenny" Johns to do the sketch as a means of examining the possibilities for the old four-door Buick left to him by his grandmother.

Looking at Kenny's sketch, with long, flowing lines, Packard taillights, '53 Buick chrome trim, a Carson top and *two* doors, Ray could see that hope springs eternal. The sketch had some lovely lines, but just how possible was this transformation? Could they take a sow's ear (this is an Iowa car) and transform it into the beautiful, sexy silk purse?

In discussing the possible transformation Kenny mentioned Merlin Berg, a man Ray was unfamiliar with. Merlin had a reputation as the restorer of

The long flowing lines of the Buick are emphasized by the Plum Wild color.

*Side chrome comes from a '53 Buick. Doors have been
stretched 7 inches in the transition from four doors to two.*

antiques. No one had ever seen a custom come out of Merlin's shop—except maybe the unfinished '55 Bel Air parked behind the shop.

A trip to Merlin's was in order and once there a discussion followed. The topics included the lines of the sketch, the methods that might be used to duplicate those lines and the cost of such an undertaking. In the end the Buick was scheduled to spend some serious time in Merlin's small shop.

Merlin started at the beginning, separating the Buick body from its frame. In the interest of reliability Merlin cut the frame and installed a subframe from a Chevrolet Nova. Where a long, straight-eight once sat, a 350 Chevy engine was installed. Instead of the whoosh of a Dyna-Flow, this Kemp would change gears with a 350 Turbo transmission. At the rear, a complete suspension and rear end from a Monte Carlo was installed.

Once the frame, suspension and engine work were completed, Merlin could turn his attention to the metalwork. Kenny's sketch showed a Buick apparently much longer and lower than stock. To duplicate the effect, Merlin added 2 inches to the front fenders. Wanting just a little more, the headlights were Frenched in the conventional way with Mercury headlight rings.

The hood was nosed and filled, and received an extra accent line on either side. The stock grille was discarded and a new, oval opening was welded up in its place. Merlin filled the oval with a '53 Chevrolet grille, modified with eleven extra teeth, new parking light assemblies on the ends and fresh chrome. Outlining the lower half of the grille, the stock bumper was simply smoothed and rechromed.

If the grille and fender modifications had been a lot of work, they were nothing compared to the work necessary from the front fenders, back. The Buick in the shop had four doors, the sketch had only two. Rather than just welding one door shut, Merlin decided to lengthen the front door and ensure the correct proportions for a two-door.

Merlin added 7 inches to the door, moving the back of the door well into the area originally occupied

Dash is mostly stock. Ray had the original Buick wheel—large, chrome and classy—adapted to the modern tilt column.

by the rear door. The rear door skin now became an extension of the rear fender and quarter panel.

While Merlin was doing all this sculpturing, he moved the line coming back from the front fender down, per Kenny's sketch. The small scoop where the lines from the front and rear fender meet was Merlin's idea and provides a nice accent. Like the front, the rear fenders were stretched—this time a full 6 inches.

The taillights were borrowed from a Packard, Frenched into the fenders, of course. The rear pan was extended and modified to meet the lines from the '55 Pontiac rear bumper. When Ray saw the car, partly finished, he thought it was fine except for the trunk lid. Unlike the line from the hood, the trunk fell away

Visual harmony. It's hard to find any part of Ray and Myrna's Buick that doesn't flow with the other parts. It's a car where everything turned out just right.

too quickly and Ray asked Merlin what they could do to raise the trunk lid.

The answer was another Buick trunk lid—just the skin actually—welded to the first one. The effect is a raised trunk and a silhouette that matches that of the hood.

Before starting on the Carson top, most of the original top was cut off. With only the windshield frame left, Merlin cut the posts 3 inches before starting on construction for the new top. The bare essentials of the Carson top framework were formed by trimming and shortening the old roof with extra metal added at the rear of the new top.

Covering the top was saved for the third member of the construction committee. Jim McFall covered the padded top and did all the interior upholstery. The front buckets are from a Monte Carlo, mounted on swivel pedestals. Jim built the rear seat from scratch and covered all the seats with raspberry Naugahyde velour. To give the car a traditional look the original steering wheel, large and shiny, was adapted to the late-model tilt column. The dash too was left stock, with the addition of an air conditioning evaporator below the dash.

While it had been easy to form a consensus during most of the construction, the last decision proved to be one of the toughest: What color to paint the beautiful Buick. Myrna wanted a plum color, but exactly what shade she just couldn't say. Some of the committee members suggested using the '53 Buick side trim as a color break—in traditional custom fashion— with maybe a lighter purple below the trim?

Myrna said no, it was going to be called *Plum Wild* and would Merlin start mixing paint please. Merlin mixed and mixed. Each new shade was applied to old pieces of sheet metal so they could be examined under different types of light. Myrna and Ray dragged the ragged color samples wherever they went, examining them outside, inside and under the fluorescent lights at the auditorium.

When the correct shade was finally settled on, Merlin had just enough time to paint and finish the car for the first showing at the Lead Sled Spectacular in 1988. At the Lead Sled show, everyone seemed to

Rear fenders have been extended 6 inches and end in Frenched Packard taillights.

agree the paint color was perfect and the use of only one color gave the car a sanitary appearance.

In the end, the net result of all the decisions and all the skill is a kind of visual harmony, a car that looks great in any situation, no matter what the light or what the competition. In working together, Ray and Myrna and the three men directly responsible for the car have created a lovely shape—one that sings. These down-home folks have taken on the best of the best, and won.

In the end they built the Buick the old-fashioned way: They started with a great design, the work was carried out by skilled craftsmen and the team was held together by two very dedicated Kustom Kempers.

Garage Sanity

The shrink is in the shop

Jim Geiger spends his days as a manager, overseeing the construction of air conditioning units at the Chrysler plant in Dayton, Ohio. It's a good job, though the responsibility for keeping things on line and on time makes it a tense one as well.

Some of the guys Jim works with do a little attitude adjustment at the saloon on the way home. Others unwind with the evening TV programs. Jim's therapist is in the garage. If the day has been long and tense, Jim takes refuge in his shop: "Working on the car is a good way to unwind. Otherwise all you think about is work and that's no good. This way I've got something to look forward to on my way home and something to do when I get there."

Jim has run a variety of vehicles over the couch in his garage. There have been a number of street rods and a few old stockers in need of work. Until a few

years ago there was just one kind of car that Jim had never built.

When Jim brought the clean, stock '53 Ford Victoria home he didn't plan to build a custom. He was only going to tinker with it—but then the tinkering got out of hand. Finally he realized that, like it or not, the Ford was turning into the custom car he had always wanted.

A little planning was in order. If the Ford was going to be a custom, what kind of custom features would it have? Jim considered all the custom cars he'd seen since he was a kid and picked the features he liked the best.

At the top of the list was the near mandatory chopped top. Now Jim had never chopped a top before, but that didn't stop him. He knew a second roof was handy to have and headed for the local junkyard to cut himself a spare top. When he got there he couldn't find another '53 Ford hardtop—all he could find was a '53 convertible. They say necessity is the mother of invention: Jim went home with a complete convertible top assembly in the back of his truck.

There are a number of ways to achieve a chopped convertible top and Jim chose the one that seemed easiest. He started by cutting the top off his Ford hardtop. Next, the convertible windshield and frame were cut 3 inches and mounted to the body. Rather than try to cut the actual framework for the top and change the geometry, Jim simply mounted the top mechanism in the body 3 inches lower than stock. Of course the side glass was cut 3 inches to match the new top.

The whole thing was almost as simple as it sounds, and Jim thinks it was easier than his original plan of chopping the hardtop. There were a few snags, like making a new front bow that was thinner than the stock piece and widening all the bows 1 inch. Yet, when it was all over the Ford had a chopped convertible top that worked just as well as stock for a minimum amount of time and money.

Two-tone paint, Frenched headlights, DeSoto grille and
wire wheels give the car a traditional custom look. On the
next pages, the rear end makes this Ford look like a

Packard. Packard Clipper taillights are protected by a
Chevrolet bumper. Convertible top has been dropped 3
inches.

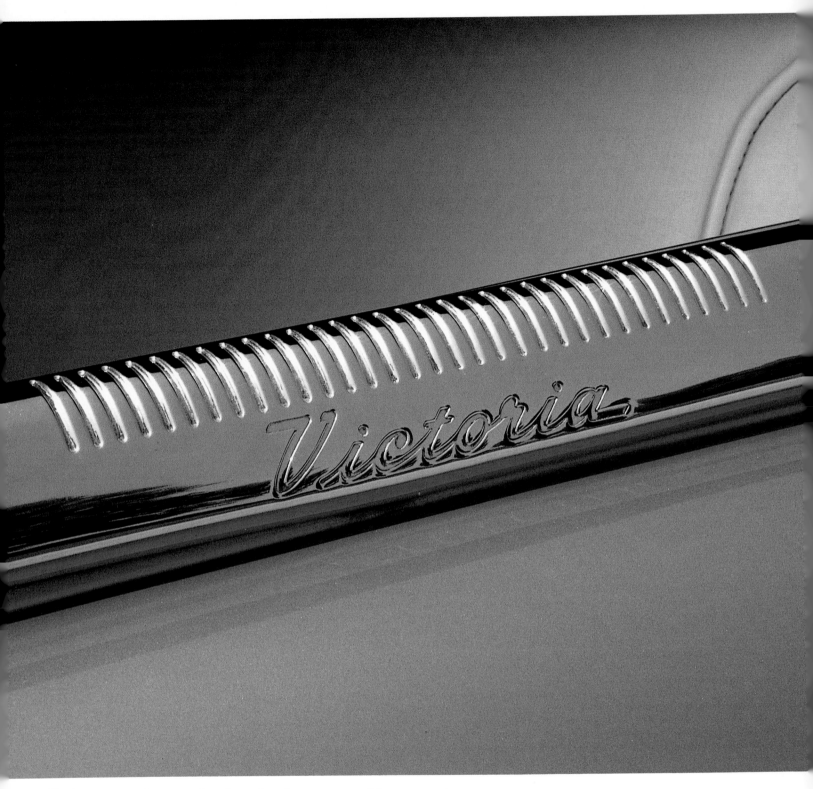

Jim's car started out as a hardtop, thus he owns one of the only Ford Victoria convertibles.

Jim's therapist is in the garage. If the day has been long and tense, Jim takes refuge in his shop

The top chop went so well Jim decided to go whole hog with the custom project. First, the body was pulled off the frame and set on one side of the shop so that some proper engine work could be done. A neighbor had a '65 Olds that became the drivetrain donor. The Olds 425 engine and automatic were installed in place of Henry's flatmotor. At the other end a Ford 9 inch rear end was mounted on 3 inch lowering blocks.

Before the body was put back on the frame Jim performed a few of those tricks he had admired on custom cars all these years. At the rear, '56 Packard Clipper taillights were mounted in the stretched Ford fenders. He admits to having second thoughts: "I thought maybe the lights were too much for the body, but I went ahead and mounted them anyway. When it was all over they looked just fine."

Scoops were added into the rear quarter panels and accented with teeth borrowed from the sides of a '53 Mercury. The simple chrome trim along the side—another standard feature on a 1950s custom—is from a '55 Pontiac Chieftain. The two-tone blue paint was applied with help from Russ Malott of Dayton.

At the front, the headlights have been Frenched and the grille opening molded into the body. The grille itself is made up of two '56 DeSoto grilles. The hood has radiused corners and 400 louvers. The front bumper is stock, minus only the visible bumper bolts.

One of the questions viewers ask most often concerns the origin of the rear bumper, the one that wraps around the Packard taillights so nicely. Jim discovered that a '56 Chevrolet bumper, narrowed 3 inches, fit perfectly.

The interior of Jim's therapeutic Ford is nearly stock. The dash is modified only by the addition of a late-model Ford tilt column and an FM stereo radio. The white rolled and pleated upholstery was stitched up by Dixon Auto Trim of Richmond, Indiana, the same people who did such a nice job with the white convertible top.

Has the Ford satisfied Jim's yearning for a custom? "Yes, I had to wait a long time but I finally got one of my own. It goes down the road great and I won

Packard Clipper taillights were popular as a replacement light assembly in custom circles but seldom seen in a '53 Ford.

the Little Guy award for Best of Show for a nonprofessional at the 1986 Lead Sled Spectacular. But the best part is when the old-timers—the guys who've been building customs for years and years—say that the lines on mine look so nice and so natural the car looks like it came off the assembly line like that."

67

Plain Jane

Black and yellow—
and flames all over

Sonny Rogers describes his Oldsmobile in the most mundane terms, usually referring to it as "just an old greasy bottomed driver."

Yet, the car Sonny describes as common has an uncommon way of stopping people in their tracks. At the Lead Sled Spectacular pedestrians would stumble through the 100 degree heat, too hot to notice any of the cars—until they came to that one crazy Oldsmobile with the great flames. One of the people who stopped to notice was Pat Ganahl, who felt the Oldsmobile was uncommon enough for a spot on the cover of an issue of *Rod & Custom*.

If Sonny seems surprised by the car's popularity maybe it's because his original plans for the car were anything but radical. It started in 1984 when a fellow from Kansas advertised a clean '55 Oldsmobile Holiday Coupe for sale. Well, Sonny and his wife Lisa left their home in Independence, Missouri, took one look and brought the Oldsmobile home.

The stock, two-tone green Oldsmobile made a great cruiser. It was a nice car with a rebuilt and warmed up Oldsmobile engine coupled to a rebuilt Hydramatic transmission. Sonny thought maybe he could sell the car, but first something had to be done about the faded paint.

Dale Markley was chosen for the repaint, to be done in the two-tone green factory colors. That might have been the end of the story except for the phone call Dale made after he started to strip the paint.

Dale explained that Sonny had to stop by the shop and see what he'd found. When Sonny asked what it was, Dale wouldn't say, insisting only that it had to be seen in person. When Sonny got to the shop he didn't see anything but an old body striped down to its birthday suit. Finally, Dale explained that it was what he *hadn't* found that seemed special. Under all that thirty-year-old paint there wasn't anything but metal—there was no rust!

Well that changed everything. If the car was that solid maybe it was a keeper. Sonny, a man friends might refer to as colorful, just couldn't see himself riding around in a stock, two-tone green Oldsmobile for any length of time. He and Dale decided that black would be a suitable color—with maybe just a few tricks to set the car off. When Sonny left the shop he gave Dale a free hand in finishing the car.

Dale thought maybe the Oldsmobile needed more than just fresh black paint. Knowing Sonny to be an old fan of custom cars, Dale and crew took the liberty of sending the hood out for louvers and knocking off the door handles.

When Sonny returned to Dale's shop five months later he discovered that the clean Oldsmobile he brought in had been transformed into a mild custom, beautiful and black. The next step was the flames— and nearly the end of Sonny's fine custom.

Dale sent the Oldsmobile out to another shop for the flame job. After hearing only vague excuses for a number of months, Sonny made a personal visit to check on the car's progress. What Sonny found turned his stomach. The flame job had gone badly. So badly

Late-afternoon sun provides flattering light for Sonny's bright, flamed Oldsmobile. Although it might be the right vintage, this is not your father's Oldsmobile.

Car is filled with subtle details, opposite, like the blue-dot lights and Frenched power antenna.

Flames were done first in yellow, then gradually fogged-in with shades of red, one flame at a time. Blue borders help each lick stand apart from the next.

that Sonny simply took the car home and parked it in a dark corner of his garage. All plans for finishing the car were put on hold for nearly a year.

Finally, with a gentle prod from Lisa, Sonny made plans to salvage the paint job as best he could. On the weekend Sonny set aside for undertaking the salvage operation, an old friend showed up and made the job much easier. Dale Reynolds is a car guy. More important at this point, Dale was a representative for Sherwin Williams paint company.

Together they looked over the once beautiful Oldsmobile. The car was covered with multiple colors

Though the car seems radical, the body panels are nearly all stock. Strong custom flavor is provided by black paint, great flames and unusual wheels.

Mississippi River bridge in Davenport, Iowa (scene of Lead Sled Spectacular 1989), makes a fitting backdrop for a colorful old Oldsmobile, opposite.

*Power front seat is from a Cadillac, bright-colored
upholstery mirrors exterior. Chrome dash insert marks the
Olds as a car of the 1950s when chrome was king.*

and layers of overspray. In places, the black had been sanded through to the primer. The flames, while laid out nicely, were a hodgepodge of mismatched colors, poorly painted in a dusty shop.

The two men started by cleaning the overspray from the glass and as much of the black paint as possible. Next, they were able to spot in new, black acrylic enamel in the areas where it was sanded down to the primer. Repairing the flames was left for last. Sonny started with bright yellow as a base and then fogged in the red, one flame at a time. The blue details are all that is left from the original flame work.

Before reinstalling the trim, a special Sherwin Williams clear coat was applied. Almost like a clear with a metal flake, the top coat contains very nicely ground mica in a gold color. The net result is a great shine, gold highlights in bright light and protection for the flame job.

Looking again like it might someday be a great car the Oldsmobile needed only finishing, a new interior, door solenoids and a lot of things that can't be seen.

All the chrome was sent out to A and A Plating in Independence for a fresh shine. Sonny installed the door solenoids, including a neat trick learned years ago. In order to make sure the door would open when the button is hit, he installed a valve spring into the door near the hinge. When the door is closed the spring is compressed, when you trip the solenoid the door jumps open with authority.

The interior is stock Oldsmobile except for the front seat, a power unit from a '67 Caddy. The new upholstery and bright colors are the work of Mick's Upholstery in Blue Springs, Missouri. Under the dash is an old add-on air conditioning evaporator with period correct heavy steel housing and chrome vents.

One of the car's most unusual features is the wheels. Sonny wanted something a little different; he liked the idea of wire wheels but they're hardly unique. What is unique are wire wheels with powder-coated yellow spokes and the chrome caps.

When it was all over Sonny and Lisa began taking the car to a variety of shows. Everywhere they went the Oldsmobile got great reviews. The more they drove it the more fun they had and the more events they

Sonny Rogers explains the finer points of laying down a nice set of flames.

went to. In 1989 they put over 6,000 miles on the car going from show to show. Sonny explained that this last season with the other Kustom Kempers is the best summer they've enjoyed for many years: "It's something about these old cars. They seem to attract a really nice bunch of people. The cars are the initiative, but then by God you run into so many nice people it's unbelievable."

What started out as the repainting of an old Oldsmobile has turned out to be much more. The Oldsmobile has turned into a noteworthy car. Sonny may not understand why, but he's got to admit that this is one crazy, colorful, crowd-pleasing Oldsmobile with the best flames this side of the hereafter.

Little Deb's Valentine

Finding true love in the garage

When Daryl Lewis found the '60 Chevrolet sitting in a cornfield he wasn't looking for a custom car. He didn't even like the looks of the car. He was just looking for a project, a father-son kind of project. Something he and his son could work on together in the evenings and weekends. The deal was this: If son Darren would work on the car with Dad, he could have it when they were through.

So Daryl inquired of the cornfield's owner and discovered that the Chevy could be had for free, but he had to buy the body parts that were stacked in the barn.

Daryl loaded up the free car and $500 worth of parts and headed for home. The parts included new front fenders and rear quarter panels. It seems the

original fenders were rotted away above the headlights and the quarters were rusted off all the way up to the chrome strip. Once they had it home, Daryl and son started by striping off the chrome and bumpers, and then trimming off what little was left of the original quarter panels.

The father-son project went along just fine that first summer but the project they tackled was a big one. In addition to fenders and quarters there were rear floor pans to fabricate and install, a door to repair and new window glass to install. Like a lot of sixteen-year-olds, young Darren gradually began to think that dates and football games were more important than Chevrolets—especially when the Chevrolet in question was scattered across the shop in a million pieces.

By the second year the restoration was progressing but without a theme. Daryl continued to hone his newfound skills as a welder and body man, though he wondered what he was going to do with the car. By this time Daryl's wife Debby had become involved in the project and had a few ideas of her own.

Debby pointed out that the car was built the same year they met at the Valentine's Prom. She went on to suggest red as the final color, reminded Daryl that they wanted a custom car anyway and finally suggested that some kind of wild Valentine theme could pull the project back together. Thus the car became *Little Deb's Valentine*, a wild, red custom Chevrolet.

Finishing the car took a total of three years. After grafting on new quarters and front fenders, Daryl had a lot to learn about finish work. He explains that the entire family—Debby, Darren and Darcy (the dog's name is Dandy)—became very proficient with 400 grit paper wrapped around a sanding block.

Daryl painted the car himself with Porsche Indian red and then turned it over to Iowa's best known pinstriper—Kenny Johns—for the wild flames and pinstriping. The interior, complete with red and white

Deb's little custom is anything but subtle. Wild flames were done by M. K. "Kenny" Johns, Porsche Indian red paint applied by the owner. On the next pages, '59 Caddy taillights, cruiser skirts, spotlights and Lakes pipes mark this Chevy as a custom. Under the hood lies a period-perfect 348 ci V–8.

The entire family became proficient with 400 grit sandpaper wrapped around a sanding block

hearts, was stitched up by Mike Lowry from Durant, Iowa.

After three years of sweat and toil Daryl and Debby took *Little Deb's Valentine* on the road. This was the custom car they had always wanted. It turned a lot of heads and it ran just fine—until a truck tried to drive over Daryl's new front fenders.

First the good news; no one was hurt. The bad news included a crunched hood and fender. Because of the flame job the entire car would have to be repainted. That was two years ago. After repairing their baby, Daryl and Debby are back on the road.

Their Chevrolet has come a long way: from cornfield to custom, from being a father-son project to being a great husband-wife project—and the best Valentine's present either one of them had ever had.

Valentine theme runs strong here, opposite. Red and white and bright, interior seems gaudy and great.

Pinstriping and detail paint explain the theme of Deb and Darryl's very red Chevrolet.

81

A Tale of Two Mercurys

The greatest shape of all —the '49-'51 Merc

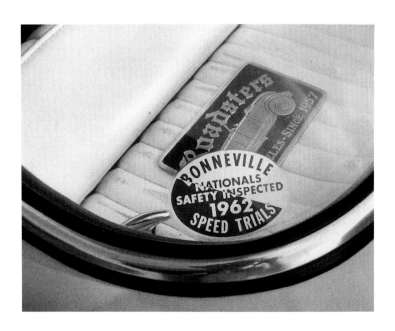

Of all the cars that customizers altered over the years, none seem more popular than the '49 through '51 Mercury. When George and brother Sam Barris built the '51 Merc for Bob Hirohata in 1953, they were on the edge of a wave, a wave of popularity that is still sweeping the country. Thirty-seven years later, in 1989, over 400 of the wonder cars appeared at the James Dean Memorial run. The Mercury shape is so enduring that Gene Winfield produces a complete "glass" body for customizers tired of fighting rust.

What's presented here are *two* Mercurys. One of these cars dates to the mid 1950s, while the other was finished in the summer of 1989. While both follow an essentially traditional theme, one carries all the latest in high-tech building trends while the older car represents the cutting edge—of thirty years ago. The two cars represent a study in contrasts and similarities.

Fred Steele's Merc

The yellow Mercury rolled off the assembly line in 1950. By the mid 1950s the car was in the hands of a young enthusiast, Paul Vigilant of Saddle Brook, New Jersey. Paul was the recent graduate of a body shop class at the local vo-tech. For years he'd been reading the West Coast magazines and for years he'd been aching to have a Merc of his own.

The car he built was a radical custom for its day. Both bumpers were replaced with elaborate rolled pans. Lincoln quad lights were installed in the front fenders and the top was cut 4 inches. Despite all the work and sweat the car slipped out of Paul's hands and passed through a series of owners, starting in about 1965.

The years were not kind to Paul's pride and joy. By 1974 the car was spied sitting outside of the Total Performance shop in Wallingford, Connecticut. The man who spotted the old hulk was Fred Steele. Intimately acquainted with old Mercurys, Fred stopped to look the car over. There was no engine or transmission. The custom front sheet metal had disappeared—replaced by a rusty front clip. There was no interior, and a vise grip served as a steering wheel. But the essentials of Paul's earlier work were intact and the quality of that work was still evident.

In 1974 the custom movement was still comatose, a hibernating bear unable to arise from the long winter's sleep. Fred was just a little ahead of the pack and immediately asked the boys what they wanted for the old Merc. The reply was $1,000, and Fred soon had the Merc at home. As he explains: "A top chop at that time was $2,500 and a decent old Merc was about $1,500 so I thought the car was a bargain."

Fred spent the next six months collecting tin, things like fenders, trim pieces and bumpers. With a trunk full of parts Fred delivered his baby to Kurt's Auto Body in Hooksett, New Hampshire, where the actual work of restoring the Merc was performed.

The shop took a conservative approach, repairing things that needed repair while leaving untouched the areas that didn't. The rolled pan in the rear was badly

Two cars very alike and yet very different. Jimmy's car, foreground, was built recently and might be considered high tech. Fred's yellow Mercury was built in the mid 1950s and rebuilt in 1975, along traditional lines both times.

Mellow yellow Merc has the right 1950s look: fender skirts, no taillights, chopped top and low to the ground.

*"A top chop at that time was $2,500 and a
decent old Merc was about $1,500, so I
thought the car was a bargain"*

damaged, so they removed it and went back to stock.
The original top chop was done with high quality
work, using hammer-welds all the way around, and
was left intact. The style of the car is traditional
1950s, with Frenched headlights, stock grille, minimal
chrome, and skirts in back.

By December 1975 Fred had his Merc back, all
straight and clean, with fresh yellow paint and still no
motor. Fred filled the underhood vacancy with a low-
mile, Chevy 350 engine and 350 transmission. It's
interesting to note that the small-block Fred installed
is the fourth engine to sit under the Merc's hood: it
came with a Flathead, Paul put in a Merc overhead-
valve V-8 and a later owner put in a Chrysler Hemi.

When Paul built the car in the 1950s, he lowered
it by "kicking" the frame at the rear and reversing the
spindles at the front. Fred left all this work intact,
installing a 9 inch Ford rear end in place of the
Mercury's own and performing mechanical repair as
needed.

By the summer of 1976 Fred's Merc was ready to
roll, except for the interior. Now Fred had been
planning a trip to Tulsa for the Street Rod Nationals.
Of course he wanted to drive the Merc, and the
unfinished interior gave him an idea. The trip to Tulsa
was made via San Francisco to visit friends, and via
Tijuana where a new, white tuck and roll interior was
installed for $166.

Today the Merc is driven to KKOA events like
Gettysburg and an occasional Sunday afternoon
cruise. Though he's had the Merc some fifteen years,
Fred is just as excited about it as he was during his
first summer with the car. While it may not be cutting
edge technology, the Merc is the car kids in high
school dreamed of owning. At least one of those kids
remembers the dreams, and enjoys the Merc each time
he drives it.

Jimmy Hendrickson's Merc

Jimmy Hendrickson's story—and Mercury—are a
little different. While the car displays a traditional
look, the underpinings are modern and high tech.
Examining this recently completed Mercury in light of
Fred Steele's much earlier car becomes a study in

*The '51 Ford taillights have been Frenched into the rear
fenders in traditional custom fashion.*

evolution—a look at where the custom movement has
been in thirtysome years.

Joe Maneri built Jimmy's Merc, known as *Angel
Eyes*. He and Jimmy set out to build a traditional Merc
with all the latest tricks. The look of the car is straight
out of the 1950s, with a 4 inch chop, '53 Buick side
trim, two-tone paint and Lake pipes.

Jimmy had seen a lot of Mercs and wanted his to
be somehow different. What's different is the full
hardtop treatment, without even a chrome channel
like the Hirohata car. To cap it off, all the windows roll
up and down—at the touch of a button. *Angel Eyes* is
one of the first to exhibit this combination of features.

The front sheet metal is different too; the
headlights are Frenched in standard style but instead

From the front this Merc might have rolled out of a James Dean movie. Grille and bumper are stock, headlights have been Frenched, pinstriping is simple and clean.

Though carrying the traditional touches like Lakes pipes and cruiser skirts, Jimmy's Merc is a very modern car.

Center post removal creates full hardtop effect and sets this Merc apart from most others.

Jimmy at the wheel. Angel Eyes *uses trim from a '53 Buick for the color break. Paint has hidden scallops that only show up in a certain light, like this late-afternoon shot.*

While the car displays a traditional look, the underpinnings are modern high-tech

of an Oldsmobile or DeSoto grille this Merc has a two-piece grille assembly from a '55 Dodge.

At the rear, *Angel Eyes* continues the traditional look with bubble skirts and '51 Ford lights Frenched into the fenders. The paint above the Buick chrome spear is Candy Apple red over a Shimrin silver base, with hidden scallops. Below the spear the paint is pink over white pearl, with flakes in the pearl.

Perhaps one of the biggest differences between old customs and new is in the drivetrain. Jimmy's car follows the modern subframe route. When Joe built the car he cut the Merc frame at the firewall and spliced in a front frame clip from a late-model GM car. The subframe offers power steering, disc brakes, modern suspension, a great ride and motor mounts for a small-block V-8—a combination that's hard to beat.

The Chevrolet small-block in this Merc is healthy: a 355 ci motor built by McBetts Racing with the emphasis on real world low- and mid-range power.

Most of the interior follows the same traditional theme as the body style with red and white upholstery on stock Merc seats and panels. The dash has been reworked, however: five individual gauges and the FM stereo tape deck are mounted in a polished panel that runs across the dashboard.

In the end, Jimmy's car is a traditional Merc with some modern updates. The look is early 1950s, the power windows and subframe are definitely late 1980s. This could be the car Paul Vigilant would build if he were thirty-five years younger.

A study in similarities and contrasts, the two cars presented here are testimony to the staying power of both custom cars and the Mercury design. Spanning thirty-five years, these two cars are ultimately more alike than they are different. The differences represent progress and change—a healthy sign that the custom movement is alive and well. The similarities provide

Attention to detail: while most antennas are Frenched, Joe went one step further. On the next pages, Angel Eyes from the front. Grille is an unusual choice, from a '55 Dodge. Note twin power antennas, Frenched into the body, of course. Hidden scallops are more hidden from this angle of view.

continuity, a tie between then and now. It's a bond that makes the hobby stronger—the ability for customs and Kustom Kempers to go forward without forgetting their past.

Harold's Pride and Joy

European styling meets American know-how

Harold Olson loved cars and he loved car events. A regular at most KKOA events, he represented California well as the state KKOA colonel. Harold was always there, quick with a smile, happy to cooperate, always willing to help in any way he could. It's sad to say, but Harold won't be on the KKOA summer circuit. Harold passed away in late 1989.

Harold always had nice vehicles, whether it was the new, Chevy duallie used as a tow vehicle or a professionally built custom. During the summer of 1989 Harold was usually seen near a recently completed project. The car he so proudly displayed was a '48 Chevrolet Fleetline—an especially lovely custom, even by Harold's standards.

The Chevrolet was purchased as a mild custom from a man in Washington state. Harold intended to change the Chevrolet from mild to wild. Before the serious work could begin, however, a planning session was held with two old friends well acquainted with customs. Rod Powell is well known as a painter, and as organizer of the picnic and show he holds each year. Henry Hurlhey from Salinas, California, is known for his fine metalwork.

The car they planned would have European lines, lines like the prewar Talbots—a teardrop shape, larger at the front and tapering to the rear. This is also the shape most commonly used by the customizers of the late 1940s and early 1950s. It was Rod Powell who actually drew up the sketch, a '48 Chevrolet fastback with a dropped top that tapered back to the trunk in one smooth sweep. The sketch included a front fender line that ran all the way across the door until it merged with the rear fender.

Harold took the Chevrolet to James Bushaw for some chassis updates before any customizing began. Jim installed a front frame clip from a '69 Firebird and a rear end from a '55 Chevy. The rear end was mounted on lowering blocks and the frame was C'ed so the Chevy could ride nice and low.

The engine Jim installed is a heavy hitting small-block from Ryan Falconer Racing in Salinas, California. Engine details include high-compression pistons, ported heads and the full blueprint, balance and dyno treatment. Transmitting all that horsepower to the rear is a rebuilt 350 Turbo transmission.

With the chassis work finished and Rod Powell's sketch in hand, the Chevy was taken to Henry's shop so the serious metalwork could commence.

Achieving the correct profile, the sweeping line that runs from the windshield to the rear bumper, was dependent on the top chop. Henry took 3 inches out of the front windshield post and 5 inches from the rear. In order to bring the trunk lid forward and down to meet the newly cut top, metal had to be sectioned from the area between the trunk lid and the top of the rear fenders. To keep the car as clean as possible the window post was eliminated altogether, creating a true hardtop. When the new windshield glass was cut, it was cut to be V-butted at the center seam.

Making the front fenders and doors follow the sweeping lines of the sketch involved some metal

The lines on Harold's fine Fleetline seem to flow from front to back without interruption. Design goal was a car that tapered to the rear like a prewar Talbot.

Great attention to detail in the rear. Taillights have been moved to the bumper, fenders have been molded to the body, skirts fit flush.

Clean sweep of metal running across the door from the front fender to the rear fender was borrowed from a '47 Buick Roadmaster, opposite.

Henry Hurlhey, the Chevrolet's builder, eliminated the center post for true hardtop look, on the previous pages. Top has been cut more at the rear for the correct tapering profile. With the exception of the tilt column and laminated knobs, on this page, dash is mostly stock Chevrolet. Front buckets are from a Riviera, upholstery by Bob Sipes.

Whether the styling influence is European or early custom doesn't really matter—the effect is dramatic and unique

exchange with other vehicles. The most extensive change happened to the doors where the Buick fade-away panels from a '47 Roadmaster were trimmed and welded to the Chevrolet doors. The Chevrolet front fender was modified at the rear edge to match the fade-away panels on the doors. To complete the sweeping line, the small pods just ahead of the rear fenders were transferred from the Buick as well.

At the front of the car the headlights and parking lights were both Frenched into the fender. Henry made the large oval grille by first forming the oval. Next, the opening was outlined and filled with the trim and bars from two '46 Chevrolet grilles.

Trying to stay true to their own design and minimize the copying of "standard" custom tricks, Henry and crew filled the hood and then created scoops on the sides rather than louvers. The rear corners of the hood have been radiused as well.

To clean up the rear sheet metal, Henry removed the taillights entirely and molded the fenders to the body. The missing lights were built into the bumper guards with handmade lenses. The bumper itself has been given the smooth treatment and moved three inches closer to the body.

Once the body work was completed Harold took his pride and joy to Bob Sipes of Grandview, Missouri, for the upholstery work. Bob installed the Riviera front seats and constructed the rear seat from scratch. The upholstery is done in a white pearl with orange piping and accents. The dashboard is nearly all stock, with a modern tilt column.

The only thing left was the paint. Harold and Henry chose a two-step process, using a base coat of Clear Pearl Candy Tangerine covered by black lacquer. The paint was applied by Henry's assistant, Adolfo Martinez, over a period of thirty days.

The finished product of all this skill and TLC is an

Harold looks out proudly from his recently completed MERCETR at the Lead Sled Spectacular 1989.

outstanding car. Whether the styling influence is European or early custom doesn't really matter, the effect is dramatic and unique.

Harold and crew created quite a car, one of the best. The future is uncertain, though there are rumors that family members will continue to show the car. That would certainly fit both the character of the car and the man who had it built.

99

Paint finish is almost too good to be true—reflections are from the tent where Harold kept his pride and joy during the Lead Sled Spectacular 1989, opposite.

Front headlights and parking lights have been Frenched per standard custom practice. Grille is unusual, formed from two '46 Chevrolet grilles.

High-Flying Buick

A four-holer built to fly

If this '60 Buick looks low and long and almost airplane-like, maybe it's because Hubert Harness, the Buick's owner, works at the Cessna airplane plant in Wichita, Kansas. If the work you see on the Buick is of high quality it's probably because Hub is a welder at Cessna, and quality work is the only kind he knows how to do.

Hub is a quiet man, never prone to bragging about his abilities or the fact that he did nearly all the work on the car himself. But if you ask, Hub will explain in his soft Kansas drawl that the car started out as a decent stocker with a bad transmission. He goes on to explain why he chose a '60 Buick: "I wanted a sixties body style, something with radical lines. My plan was to build a mild custom, no chopped top or any of that. The car had to be something different, one that hadn't been built before. I didn't really have a plan drawn out, I had most of it in my head, the car seemed to come together as I built it."

The building began at the rear where headlight housings, the kind that might be used on a '32 Ford, were modified to accept two '59 Caddy taillight lenses. After the housings were modified to suit, Hub welded them to the car. By forming the housings on the bench and then welding them to the car, Hub got a near perfect fit and didn't need much body filler.

The rest of the car followed from the rear end: most of the modifications are amplifications of the stock lines and many incorporate bullets in some form.

The quad headlight housings were formed from two large-diameter tubes joined in a housing of Hub's own manufacture. The housing leaves the headlights in a tunnel and pulls the front end some 5 inches forward.

The grille is based on a '58 Ford grille with—count 'em—twenty-five bullets. Above the grille the hood has been "pancaked" or separated from its front lip. In the center is a small scoop built by hand and housing another small bullet.

It's hard to have a Buick without port holes, though these don't look like anything to come from Detroit. Formed from aircraft strut tubing cut at a 45 degree angle, the ports are joined to the fender and each hole holds its own bullet. On the left fender the power antenna is nicely Frenched into the body, with a neat cavity where the antenna goes through the crease in the body panel.

The body creases themselves, with their crisp, sculptured lines, appear heavily modified. In reality the sides were modified only slightly: the trim was removed, and another scoop was formed near the rear of the car to tie the upper and lower body lines together.

One of the problems with doing something different, like customizing a Buick, is the difficulty in finding custom parts. For chrome wheels, Hub had to buy four wheels with the correct bolt pattern and then mill the center hole large enough to fit the Buick hub. There was still a clearance problem, solved by removing a little metal from the large fins on the brake drums. The chrome "spiders" are old Cal Custom pieces found at a swap meet.

Built entirely at home by a non-professional, this is the wildest Buick to come down the road in a long, long time. Design follows and exaggerates the stock Buick lines.

Interior uses four Chevrolet bucket seats. Top of dash has been eliminated, replaced by individual gauges, each in its own chrome housing.

Six two-barrel carburetors feed the Nail-Head Buick V–8. Use of chrome is extensive. Note air conditioner compressor, hood hinges, wiper motor, water pump and so on. On the next pages, as if a '60 Buick wasn't long enough to start with, this one has been extended on both ends. Radical port holes and Frenched antenna by the owner.

A welder at the Cessna plant in Wichita, Kansas, Hubert did nearly all the work on this radical Buick himself.

"I didn't really have a plan drawn out, I had most of it in my head. The car seemed to come together as I built it"

Custom cars are averse to any kind of unnecessary bumps, things like chrome and door handles. In true Kemp fashion, Hub threw the door handles away and electrified the doors. The windows got the power treatment too, but only after adapting power assemblies from a Cadillac for the vent and rear windows, and a Chevrolet for the door windows.

Never content to leave anything alone, Hub took the top off the dash and mounted the gauges in five separate housings. The Stewart-Warner speedo is mounted in a spotlight housing, while the smaller gauges are mounted in Harley-Davidson accessory taillight housings. Seating is handled by four Chevrolet Super Sport bucket seats. The two-tone upholstery seen on the seats, door panels and headliner was done by Scott Downing.

While the car is named *Cinnamon*, the actual bronze color is Corvette Russet Poly, a lacquer with a polyurethane clear coat. There were only two major operations Hub didn't do, the upholstery and the finish paint. The Corvette lacquer was applied by Justin "Bondo" Fields from Hutchinson, Kansas.

After a year and a half of hard work the Buick was ready for the Lead Sled Spectacular. Spectators at the Lead Sled show surrounded the car and heaped praise on the humble builder. It seemed Hub had succeeded. The Buick is mild, wild and certainly different from anything seen before.

Front end features a pancaked hood, extended headlight housings and a handmade grille with 25 chrome bullets.

From this perspective the Buick seems like a radical, powerful cruiser. Headlight housings were made from large-diameter tubing joined together to form a housing.

Handbuilt taillight housings seem a natural extension of the fender, opposite. Taillight lenses are from a '59 Cadillac—what else? Quadrasonic exhaust tips were built by the owner.

Another *Bad Boy*

Some kids never learn their lessons

Each custom car is unique, though some are more unique than others. One of the most uncommon cars seen recently is the '50 Oldsmobile fastback belonging to "Big George" Greenwalt of Grant, Florida. An avid car nut and custom freak, George has owned a variety of cars. Before building *Bad Boy II* there was a '50 Ford business coupe with a very serious small-block Chevy motor, tubs and enormous rear tires. While the original *Bad Boy* was a great ride and fun to drive, George wanted something more unusual.

The one body style that appealed to George with both strong lines and a seldom seen status was the '50 Olds fastback. Even while building the Ford pro-business coupe, George remembers: "The idea of a chopped, '50 Olds two-door had always appealed to me. One day I was talking to John McNealy [long-time professional car builder and customizer] and John told me he had chopped one years ago. John was pretty sure the car never got finished."

When George finally found the Oldsmobile that had been chopped eleven years earlier, it was a basket case. A project that had been sold and sold again, though somehow never finished. The body was all there, though in pretty rough shape. There was no glass and no interior. A 472 ci Caddy motor had been installed but didn't run. After some negotiating, George bought the car and loaded it on a trailer for the tow home.

The first step was the motor. The Caddy engine was considered, but the more George thought about it the more he wanted the new fastback to be fast. Fast like the first *Bad Boy*, fast like serious street racers, fast like 500 horsepower.

Soon an old Chevrolet Suburban showed up in the driveway and before long the Suburban's big-block was mounted to an engine stand in the shop. When George builds a car, he farms out most of the body work but keeps the mechanical work for himself. The Chevy 454 ci mill was completely disassembled before being sent out to be cleaned and bored.

Before reassembly, everything was balanced. George installed new 0.030 inches over, TRW forged pistons, stock rods and a steel crankshaft. A Crane cam operates the roller rockers. The stock heads were treated to a three-angle valve job, stainless valves and cc'ed combustion chambers, all done by American Cylinder in Vero Beach, Florida.

The big-block was bolted to a rebuilt 350 Turbo tranny, sporting a 3000 rpm stall converter. After some deliberations, the idea of installing the engine in the stock frame rails lost out to the more modern subframe concept. Tony's Texaco cut the frame at the firewall and grafted on a Camaro frame section complete with power steering and disc brakes. With the high-horse motor, a new set of rear gears seemed the only answer. George chose the bullet-proof 9 inch Ford rear end, with Detroit Locker Positraction and 3.70 gears.

Once the driveline was installed, George spent a number of evenings driving up and down the streets near his house in the fastback—with no windows, one

The nice thing about customs, whenever you think you've seen them all, along comes something completely different.

This '50 Olds fastback makes an uncommon, and very clean, custom.

bucket seat and a two-gallon gas tank sitting on the floor beside him. "I wanted to get all the bugs out of the engine and driveline before I started on the rest of the car," he remembers.

A local glass shop installed new glass, including rear side windows that crank up and down. Finally,

with a drivetrain and glass installed it was time to think about smoothing out some of the bumps in the two-door body.

Charlie Butterfield is both a talented body man and a good friend to George. With the car in primer, George and Charlie went over it in chalk, George

113

Rear of the Olds carries Corvette bumpers and Corvette taillight assemblies.

marking areas where he wanted scoops or a radiused fender lip.

George and Charlie agreed that the headlights should be Frenched and scoops opened up underneath. At the same time they tried to keep the headlight and the area below it looking uniquely like an Oldsmobile. The front end treatment was finished off with a Corvette grille and a bumper that was originally the bottom half of a '53 Buick bumper.

In order to provide sufficient tire clearance, the front fender lip has been radiused. The rear fenders have been molded to the body for the smooth look and feature a recess at the rear to accommodate the

Corvette bumper sections. The taillights too are from a Corvette and they fit the fender line so well it looks like all '50 Oldsmobiles came this way—or should have.

After some finishing work the car was taken to Fred's Auto Body for paint. It might be instructive to quote from the tech sheet George sent regarding the outcome of the paint job: "After 13 months and a lot of hard work and frustration on both Fred and Charlie's part the *Bad Boy II* was ready to paint. Wouldn't you know . . . after a near perfect paint job by Fred and striping completed by Son of Sign the clear was ready to go on. You guessed it—the paint

The more George thought about it, the more he wanted the new fastback to be fast. Fast like the first **Bad Boy,** *fast like serious street racers, fast like 500 horsepower*

lifted and wrinkled. Soooo back to sanding, sanding, sanding."

By the time the car was ready for paint again, George had experienced a change of heart. The new color would be yellow—with new, wraparound graphics. The graphics are rather innovative, designed by George and crew late one night after too much Scotch. In the harsh light of day they still liked the design but couldn't agree on a color. Finally it was Sally, Fred's wife, who suggested the magenta. George thought magenta meant pink and pointed out the fact that he's far too macho a guy for any pink highlights. Fred had to spray in part of the design to make George understand that this really wasn't *pink* and that no matter, it looked great with the yellow.

The interior of George's car was done by Jeff Driscoll of Melbourne, Florida. The front seats came from a Mercedes while the rear seat was made to fit. The dashboard with its tunneled gauges and wood trim is more work from the talented hands of John McNealy. Below the dash are mounted the small vents for an Air-Tique air conditioning unit. Set higher in the dash is a modern FM stereo tape player.

Bad Boy II was finished in time for the 1989 season. By the end of that season George had accumulated more than 7,000 miles on the yellow streak. When asked why he enjoys the car so much, George is quick to reply, "It's fast, it rides like a Lincoln and best of all, I haven't seen another one since I built it."

Air scoop has been created and the headlight Frenched. Small pinstripe outlines the scoop. On the next pages, bad looking Oldsmobile gets its look from a chopped top, filled body seams, bright yellow paint and new-wave graphics.

Corvette taillight seems tailor-made for an Oldsmobile fender, opposite.

Despite the Corvette grille, '53 Buick bumper and scoops under the headlights, the front sheet metal retains the unmistakable look of an Oldsmobile.

What's Old Is New Again

"The look may change but the ideas are the same"

That quote comes to mind as one views Roger Jetter's '57 Chevrolet. At first it seems inappropriate to place this very modern Chevrolet among '50 Mercurys and '48 Chevrolets—cars built along traditional custom lines. Yet, what were the first customs if not radical? Haven't customs always been the expression of an individual—one person's way of seeing an automobile?

Roger's automotive world has always included '57 Chevrolets. At one time he owned thirty of the classic Chevy shapes. The current Kemp was given to Roger in the early 1970s by a man who owed him $160. The car was anything but cherry, a Model 210 with some crunched front sheet metal. Roger replaced the sheet metal and put the Chevrolet on the road.

After driving it for a number of years, Roger got the bug to build a custom. Out came the stock grille, in went a '54 Chevy grille. Other traditional custom features were added along with a rebuilt 250 cube, six banger. Roger used his new custom as a daily driver,

120

putting over 130,000 miles on the clock during the next five years.

By the time the Chevrolet was ready for its third incarnation Roger was ready for a change. He explains that "there are so many '57s that I wanted to build one that was different from all the rest."

Before starting, Roger—who makes part of his income as a graphic artist—drew up a plan. The idea was a '57 Chevy that retained the look of a '57 without looking like everyone else's.

The first thing Roger tackled was mechanical repair. After pulling out the tired six-cylinder, a 400 ci Chevy small-block was obtained. After a thorough rebuild the V-8 was installed and mated to a 400 Turbo tranny.

With the major mechanical work finished it was time to start on the more interesting and challenging metalwork. The fins and taillights were first. The edges of the fins were mocked up from cardboard. Once the shape was determined, the actual metal was bent from 18 gauge sheet steel in a local sheet metal shop. Roger did all his own welding and body work.

To create the oval housing for the twin taillights, Roger started with round rod bent to shape and covered with sheet steel. Set inside are two aftermarket Corvette light assemblies. The rear bumper was borrowed from a Maverick, minus the ends. Before installation it was smoothed and powder coated to match the rest of the car. Roger formed the pan below the bumper by hand.

Moving forward, Roger did the necessary removal of the door handles, installing electric solenoids in their place. In tune with the modern theme, the vent windows were eliminated and tinted glass was installed in all the side windows. The hood had been louvered during construction phase number two. Looking for new hood treatment, the hood bullets were removed and the area filled to provide a unique mounting point for two 400 emblems.

The headlights have been Frenched and the effect is so subtle it's easy to miss but the lights have been placed 2 inches back into their housings. The front

Roger's Chevy carries the unmistakable profile of a '57 Chevrolet—with some very unique features.

Fins have been brought to a point at their edges with sheet metal. Bumper was originally on a Maverick, trimmed to fit and powder coated to match the rest of the car.

bumper is stock Chevrolet, minus the two Cadillac-type orbs on each side. Roger built the air dam to follow the contours of the bumper.

The grille is rather unique, created from many long pieces of 1 inch, flat aluminum stock. First, the multiple layers were drilled and bolted together with spacers between each layer. Next, the assembled, stacked block of aluminum was taken to a machinist who milled enough from each side to create the V in the center. Finally, the edges were trimmed so it would fit the grille opening.

Once the bulk of the body work was finished there was the trim and interior to consider. Inside, the high-tech Chevrolet is upholstered in two tones of grey velour. The front bucket seats are from a '64 Super Sport, the console between them is handmade. As a special touch, the dash and inside window trim are covered with dove grey leather.

The new-wave graphics, done in magenta and blue, are Roger's design. The two-tone stripes are seen both inside and outside the car, running along the dash, through the upholstery, over the headliner and under the hood and trunk as well.

The street sneaker logo was used on another of Roger's cars (Yup, another '57 Chevy) and transferred to this one. The shoes are a nice touch; the magenta laces are almost too much.

In the end Roger has created a clean, unique '57 Chevrolet. Not a traditional custom, yet by building this unusual car Roger has gone forward into the past. The past, where daring young men worked to create shapes that were better than those from Detroit and different from everyone else's.

Even non-traditional customs carry standard custom tricks, like this Frenched headlight. A 400 emblem is mounted in place of the factory bullet. On the next pages, this '57 started out as a 210 model, the middle of the line. Graphics were designed by the owner.

Is it possible to have a '57 Chevy without fuzzy dice? Interior follows exterior theme—modern but not too radical. Graphics used on outside are seen on dash, front seat and headliner.

A close-up view, opposite, re-worked fins, handbuilt light housings and aftermarket Corvette light assemblies.

Air dam was built by hand and powder coated. Grille is made from many pieces of flat stock with small spacers between each one.